To Maureen
With Love and Light
Anne Merani

The School of the New Spirituality Guidebook Series
in
"Applications for Life" Study Kits
Titles based on the *Conversations with God* Series
by Neale Donald Walsch

What God Wants - Kristin Stewart
Happier than God - Linda Lee Ratto
Communion with God - Maggie Reigh, Christina Erls-Daniels
Tomorrow's God - Christina Semple
Home with God - Kimberly Darwin
CONVERSATIONS WITH GOD with Teens Guidebook - Jeanne Webster, Emily Welch
Conversations with God, Book 2 - Anne-Marie Barbier
Conversations with God, Book 3 - Alissa Goefran
Conversations with God, Book 1 - Nancy Lee Ways
Friendship with God - Donna Corso
The New Revelations - Patricia Glenn, Erma Watson

Life is our curriculum, lived in Love, Joy and Wisdom !

Each contains activities revealing new ways to think about God and fresh ways to think about education. Inspired and based upon the wildly popular NY Times best selling *Conversations with God* books, they are playful life guides with discoveries and personal enrichment that you can practice for your own growth.

What then?

You may easily use any guidebook as a workshop plan into your community. Learning, of course, is lifelong and adding your touch by teaching with the multi-sensory experiences in these guidebooks will expand your own development and those in your world. Play away and see what miracles you make.

~Linda Lee Ratto, EdM
SNS Executive Director

There are many different names for the divine source of creation: God, any other name you prefer and hold to be your truth. What you call your creative force depends upon your religion or dogma and beliefs, each is equally sacred. For the sake of continuity and consistency and while trying not to offend any person or group, we will use the term "God."

School of the New Spirituality (SNS)

New Spirituality Principles-in-Action
Guidebooks
based on
Neale Donald Walsch's
Conversations with God Book Series

Conversations with God, Book 2
Guidebook

By Anne-Marie Barbier
SNS Board of Trustees and Certified Chopra Instructor

The "New Spirituality" is a way of honoring our natural impulse toward the Divine without making others wrong for the way in which *they* are doing it."
~ **Neale Donald Walsch**

ISBN 978-0-9815206-9-8

**Library of Congress
Catalogue Information,
and
Search Engine Topics:**

1. Education, 2. Enrichment Education, 3. Heart based
Education, 4. Spiritual Education, 5. Self Esteem, 6. Character
Development, 7. Values Education

Professionally Edited by:
Helene Camp
and
Mary Lee and Ray Hammond

published by:

SNS Press
Post Office Box 622
Tyrone, Georgia 30290
United States of America

T a b l e of C o n t e n t s
Conversations with God Book 2 – A Guidebook

"Our Collective Time on the Planet"
(Chapter 5)

based on
Neale Donald Walsch's

Conversations with God Book 2
Guidebook

by Anne-Marie Barbier
SNS Board of Trustees and Certified Chopra Center Instructor

Writer's Personal Introduction: Why am I co-writing this guidebook?

by Anne-Marie Barbier

When I was a teenager, growing up in France, I lacked confidence. My internal dialogue was saying: "To be successful, you have to be beautiful, but I am ugly." This was a very stressful, counter-productive way to live.

I went to see a French doctor who taught me how to relax my body through meditation. This technique was very helpful to me and I used it on and off for twenty years. Ten years ago, I was inspired by Deepak Chopra's teaching and writings and registered for a Chopra seminar in India. To be prepared for that experience, I learned Primordial Sound Meditation. Since then, I have been practicing Primordial Sound Meditation twice daily. As I practiced my meditations, I realized I had to make some personal changes. I studied even more and read *Conversations with God,* by Neale. I soon discovered how I could live a better life filled with joy, passion, happiness, and harmony.

My life has completely changed because I *happened* to meet someone who turned out to be much more important than anyone in my life: myself. Internal shifts happened naturally and continue to shift me at all levels as I use so many techniques and tools from my in-depth studies. Friends and family have been noticing these productive, positive changes and these wonderful shifts are why I wanted to share the benefits I experienced in meditation. So I decided to become a teacher through the Chopra Center for Well Being, in California. I now teach "Primordial Sound Meditation," the "Seven Spiritual Laws of Yoga" and the "Seven Universal Laws of Success in the Workplace," and continue my life-purpose teaching by co-writing this *CONVERSATIONS WITH GOD* 2 Guidebook. I intend to guide others with this Guidebook as a School of the New Spirituality Alliance Leader with my "Applications for Life" guidebook colleagues, a group of sixteen inspirational professionals. It is my desire that you, too, will be inspired by this marvelous body of work. It is a simple and joyous way of life.

Dedications

To my family in France, who has always been so supportive of everything I have ever done in my life.

To Linda Lee Ratto, whose friendship and guidance has been a true blessing over the years.

To Neale Donald Walsch, who gave me the opportunity to co-write this guide book.

To Deepak Chopra, my beloved teacher, whose teaching has been bringing me to a higher level of consciousness every day.

To you, the reader, who is on a spiritual journey with me. When many of us think that hard work (no pain, no gain...) is what we must do to erase old thought patterns, you are taking the steps to change effortlessly. I don't believe that making inner changes must be hard work or painful. It can be a wonderful voyage. Let us begin...

Book Summary

The word God is used in this book as a reference to the Divine or the Universal energy. However, it means whatever you define as God to you.

In the introduction to *Conversations with God, Book 1,* the first book of the CWG trilogy, Neale Donald Walsch was told that *Book 2* "would deal with more global topics of geopolitical and metaphysical life on the planet, and the challenges now facing the world." And yet there is even more in this book – more about God, about life and death, relationships, good and evil, money, education, and spirituality.

What is proposed here is nothing less than a paradigm shift to change the political and spiritual constructs that human beings have manifested on this planet:

"Now is the time to *reclaim yourself.* Now is the time to see yourself again as Who You Really Are, and thus, render yourself visible again. For when you, and your true relationship with God, become visible, then We are *indivisible.* And nothing will ever divide Us again."

~ Neale Donald Walsch on the back cover of
Conversations with God Book 2

How to use this Guidebook

I advise you to read this Guidebook once straight through. Let the words seep into you. Allow your memories, thoughts and feelings to come up. Look at yourself anew simply by this first reading. Then go back and do the discovery exercises and examine how you feel. Try to focus and thoroughly address an activity at a time. Even, if you have no problem in one area, I still suggest you do the exercises. You might be surprised by what may surface. If there is an area of your life that is particularly difficult for you, do the exercises several times. The very thought process will shift your being to a new awareness.

This is a book about change. I grew up in poverty or lack consciousness, even though I had material abundance around me. I had very little self-esteem and I experienced many challenges relating with others. I remember a time when I wanted everyone else to change around me and then I thought my life would be perfect. When I finally realized that it simply does not work that way, I started shifting inside and my life changed. Now, I have created a fresh, healthy, beautiful life for myself, helping others and I no 'suffer'. Do you want to make a commitment to yourself and start changing, to feel the ease and flow of life?

Be kind to yourself as you start this journey of doing exercises in this Guidebook. You will discover new information about yourself. It may be uncomfortable or painful at times, remembering certain life events. Keep some Kleenex close by and allow yourself to cry and feel ! If you have to take a break from doing the exercises, do it. Yes do what you can to be understanding about yourself. Along the way, you will be planting some seeds in your consciousness. These seeds may take time to grow and develop. It's all right, it is OK. You don't produce a peach tree in a second.

Remember that any beliefs you have about yourself and the world, are only thoughts and you can always change them. And on he other hand, you may not agree with some of the ideas you are about to explore. You may think that some of the exercises are too simple, even elementary. Some of them may not be familiar or could even feel a bit scary. Don't worry. Give these ideas a try. They might just work for you, in Divine Timing.

When you are ready to start, get prepared:
- Read each chapter thoroughly.
- Materials needed: journal, notebooks or sketchbooks, 2-month or longer calendar. Internet access for research. Massage body oil, full length mirror, hand mirror.
- Timeframe: daily for three-to-six weeks to get optimal benefit and to create new life habits.

Conversations with God, Book Two
Guidebook

Chapter 1

SPIRITUAL CONNECTION TO THE DIVINE

Chapter 1 Summary

This chapter states that we are all creating what is happening in our lives *in union with God.* Nothing happens by accident. And to realize that we are not separate from God, we live in a new truth.

"When I say "Your will is My Will," that is not the same thing as saying My Will is your will. If you did My Will all the time, there would be nothing more for you to do to achieve Enlightenment. The process would be over. You would be already there. One day of doing nothing but My Will would bring you Enlightenment. If you had been doing My Will all the years you've been alive, you'd hardly need to be involved in this book right now. So it's clear you have not been doing My Will, In fact, most of the time you don't even know My Will."

~ Neale Donald Walsh, Chapter 1, p 5
Conversations with God Book 2

---

2 – Quotes from Other Spiritual Masters

Conversations with God books by Neale Donald Walsch are among numerous resources containing profound and life-altering spirituality principles. Most religions and numerous spiritual writers teach many similar core principles. In each chapter I provide quotes by Master teachers from across the ages and around the world.

"The material universe is the body of Nature. Since I and the Unified Field are One in our ground state, I am the witness in the Unified Field, my thoughts or mind are just a different manifestation of the same forces of Nature that we call heat, light, electricity, magnetism, and gravity. My body is just a different manifestation of the same body that I call the Universe."

~ Deepak Chopra
Everyday Immortality.

"True salvation is fulfillment, peace, life in all its fullness. It is to be who you are, to feel within you the good that has no opposite, the joy of Being that depends on nothing outside itself. It is felt not as a passing experience, but as an abiding presence. In theistic language, it is to "know God" – not as something outside you, but as your own innermost essence."

~ Eckhart Tolle
The Power of Now

3 – Principles & Objectives

Principles
(Core new ideas for the world, according to Neale Donald Walsch)

I. Chapter 1 touches on the synchronicity, or seemingly coincidence of events:

a) Miracles happen all the time.

b) We often don't see these miracles. We *decide* to observe them or to neglect them. Miracles are opportunities and may be turning points in life, or not.

II. Chapter 1 presents the concept of union with God:

a) "If you can't love yourself, you can't love anyone else." This is a universal truth.

b) Loving oneself, for many people, remains a vague notion.

c) Searching for a personal spiritual connection stirs us to our core.

d) We don't wish to have our ego act as a filter to guide us. We desire God to move with us directly, thus removing obstacles, pain or negativity. This is the Divine potential inborn within each of us.

III. Chapter 1 addresses Universal truth concepts:

a) Your higher truth derives from a state of being in which you are able to distinguish your observations from your interpretations.

b) Commitment to life-supporting choices are aligned with an expanded view of self.

c) Be in integrity of thought, word and action.

d) Truthfulness is an expression of your commitment to a spiritual life, a life beyond ego.

e) Ultimately, we recognize truth, love, and God to be different expressions of the same undifferentiated reality.

Learning Objectives:

A) You will start to connect with the source of all possibilities; this is when the magic of life happens.

B) You will start showing less judgment toward self and others; this is a new freedom.

C) You will observe your unique kind of spiritual connection to the Divine, through personal examination.

4 – Exercises

> ***Conversations with God book 2*, Chapter 1- Affirmation**
>
> **"My intention is to remove obstacles from my life to transform limitations in my physical, mental and emotional body that keep me from realizing the Divine potential inborn within me."**

1. You have opened this book to read. Is this action a coincidence?
Miracles happen all the time. Become awake to miracle moments, and your life can be changed into an awe-inspiring experience. If you ignore miracles, new opportunities are gone.

We have all been in touch with dazzling experiences. Close your eyes and take a moment to think about all the events that led you to this book.

- Did a friend or a family member tell you about this book?
- Who is this friend or family member? What is the connection between this friend or family member, you and this book?
- Or you may have walked through an aisle at the bookstore? How did you decide to go into the bookstore?
- Did an email pop into your computer, just at the right time – so now you have this book in your hand?
- Look back on your calendar. Consider the sequence of events that have truly brought miraculous people or happenings into your life. Write or perhaps sketch them in your journal.

2. Make a commitment to practice non-judgment for one hour. Don't judge anything or anyone, not even yourself. From an hour, you can increase the practice to half a day and then to a whole day.

- Be the observer of the freedom felt as a consequence of being nonjudgmental.

- Before going to sleep, review mentally your day and honor any feelings, especially notice new feelings, perhaps those of freedom. Breath-in and feel your feelings deep inside.

- If you experienced a freedom, try seeing others in the same state of being. Write down names of these people who already show non-judgment ways. These people can be your teachers.

KEY DEFINITIONS for Chapter 1:

Co-creators: being in a state of creating with the Universe as a partner and being One with everything.

Synchronicity: what most people call "luck;" it is actually our intentions being fulfilled.

5 – Summary of this chapter lesson:

Use your journal/notebook/sketchbooks for these end of chapter questions, answering them as fully as possible. Try using your senses to consider your private feelings and thoughts and ask:

- Have you been able to find a connection between a friend or family member and this guidebook? How did it make you feel?
- In what circumstance did you feel the largest fresh new sense of liberation or relief or freedom as a result of being non judgmental?
- Have you found it possible to share the experience with others? How?

Five Levels of Truth Telling

1. Tell the truth to yourself about yourself.
2. Tell the truth to yourself about another.
3. Tell the truth about yourself to another.
4. Tell the truth about another to that other.
5. Tell the truth to everyone about everything.

~ Neale Donald Walsch
Conversations with God Book 2

Chapter 2

WILLING AND EXPERIENCING

Chapter 2 Summary:

We are all conditioned to react in a certain way, based on our past experiences. We often make choices unconsciously. Yet whatever we intend to experience in our lives, dreams, goals, intentions involve a new willingness to create the inconceivable in our mind. If we are focused on new intentions, we then get back on our feet to watch what we have, rather than what we don't have. We may choose to search for opportunities to set up our intentions and make our dreams come true. Every moment is always a chance to choose.

Two key words to assess for self are reactive and creative. We can get exasperated over anything, which is a choice. Upon self-reflection most of the time, we realize later that the incident or event was not much to be concerned about ! Yet seemingly, at that moment, we had decided to make it a drama or long story. Again, choice is there, whether we are conscious or not is another story.

In our active, often dramatic world, we don't seem to have too many occasions to meditate, pray, self-reflect, or even go on a retreat where we can focus on the growth of our spirit. Yet these are excellent jumpstarts to the positive, focused process of consciously choosing your life, consciously intending a way of life that is happy, healthy and free. Neale and God talk about not making things difficult at all in life. And we can all use some ease.

> "You can tell you are on your way to mastery when you see the gap closing between Willing and Experiencing."
>
> ~ Neale Donald Walsch, Chapter 2, p.10
> *Conversations with God Book 2*

2 – Quotes from Other Spiritual Masters

"Of course, the best way to have all your intentions realized is to align your intentions with the cosmic intent, to create harmony between what you intend and what the universe intends for you. Once that congruence comes into being, you'll find the synchronicity takes on a large role in your life. The best way to create that harmony is by nurturing an attitude of simple gratitude. Acknowledge your gratitude for everything in your life. Give thanks for your place in the cosmos and for the opportunity you have to further the destiny we all share."

~ Deepak Chopra
The Spontaneous Fulfillment of Desire

Believers
"...are individuals who have made themselves available for success. It's impossible to get them to be pessimistic about achieving what they desire in their lives. Rather than using language that indicates that their desires may not materialize, they speak from an inner conviction that communicates their profound and simple knowing that the universal Source supplies everything.

~ Wayne Dyer
The Power of Intention

"...Our thoughts, our words, and deeds are the threads of the net which we throw around ourselves."

~ Swami Vivekananda
As quoted from Deepak Chopra's book "The Seven Spiritual Laws of Success"

"You are here to enable the divine purpose of the universe to unfold. That is how important you are !"

~ Eckhart Tolle
The Power of Now

3 – Principles & Objectives

Principles:

I. Intention is creation.

II. Beliefs can be non- productive and contribute to uncomfortable experiences.

III. Name your beliefs, then change begins.

IV. Limited beliefs are just choices.

V. We are choice makers for our emotions and our lives.

VI. Destructive thoughts block us from using our energy in a more powerful, constructive way, and more in the flow with the universal energy.

Learning Objectives:

A) You will set up some specific intentions or life goals.

B) You will observe positive and less-than-positive beliefs in your internal mind-dialogue which could interfere with your life events, your daily outcomes.

C) You will practice conscious choice making.

4 – Exercises

***Conversations with God book 2*, Chapter 2- Affirmation**

"I make things happen in my life. I am learning to dream the impossible. I am willing to create a habit of doing things in a new way."

---

1. Determine exactly what you want your life to be.

   Make a list of what you want to achieve, even if it is something you feel is impossible for the moment. Address the following categories:
   - Material level
   - Relationships
   - Your sense of well being, your health
   - In terms of community, society, country, do you want to help and, if so, how?
   - Spiritual level

2. Assess your beliefs

Take a note pad or use the journal pages in the back of this guidebook and clarify any positive or unconstructive beliefs you hold deeply. Try asking yourself some pointed questions. For instance, do you believe:
- That to be successful, you have to be beautiful or do you believe success is available to all people, any age, any size, any race or culture ?
- That rich people are superior or great human beings?
- That men leave you or are just as loving as any humans?
- That women get paid less or deserve success?
- That work is boring or fulfilling and enjoyable?
- That sex is dirty or a gift for two people to share?
- That failure means not being capable or is a learning experience?
- That you are always missing money or abundance is a joy to be around?
- That love is not for you or is a glorious part of life?
- That God is to fear for your sins or always supports you unconditionally?

3. Determine desired changes

Look at the list you wrote about your beliefs, and make a note of the areas that are challenging for you. Remember that, at some point in your life, someone taught you these ideas and you believed them because you just did not know better and you had no comparison. You believed 'out-of-habit' so to speak. Now, you are making yourself aware of barriers and you have a fresh new approach to choice: you can continue to do the same thing over and over, expecting a different result, or you can decide to change your internal dialogue for positive changes.
So, experiment with new trains of thought and see what happens in your daily life. Then:

a) Discuss your conclusions with someone you trust if you wish.
b) Notice and write or sketch how you feel, when a new choice brings you a new daily outcome. Be specific. New body sensations tell you things about your well-being.

4. Examine your choices

Make a list of all the important choices you have made in your life, and notice which of these choices were conscious or unconscious. Note the date and how these choices affected your life.

Next time you want to make a choice, take a moment to think about the choice you are making. The simple fact that you are making yourself aware of that choice is bringing your awareness from unconscious to conscious level.

Then, evaluate what that choice will bring to your life and those around you. Finally, again please observe what these new choices feel like. If it feels good, the choice is a right choice for you. If it feels uncomfortable, something is 'off' or perhaps wrong about the choice. It would probably be a good idea to step back from that choice and consider another choicepoint from which to decide your next steps.

KEY DEFINITIONS for Chapter 2:

Reactive: giving into emotions without reflection nor discernment

Willing: disposed or consenting with cheerful readiness.

Experiencing: the process or fact of personally observing, encountering, or undergoing something. To learn from living, feeling, touching, tasting, sensing, smelling – rather than being *told about* something.

5 – Summary of this chapter lesson:

- When making the list of what you want to accomplish, how did it make you feel? Be specific in your journal.
- After assessing your beliefs, where you surprised? What kind of emotion did it bring up?
- Do you really want to continue to live your life with those beliefs?
- You have become experienced in looking at yourself in this chapter. You have assessed how you believe and you are planning a dream to come true for yourself. How do you feel about making the changes you desire in your life?

Chapter 3

PRESENT MOMENT AWARENESS – WE ARE ALL PERFECT

Chapter 3 Summary:

We all have a tendency to live through memory and the anticipation of the future. Through this way of looking at life, we create never ending anxiety with the past and we worry about the future. We don't allow ourselves to be in the present moment.

We are all perfect the way we are. There is no evil if we look past the idea of good and bad, that is being and acting nonjudgmental in every moment.

> "There is no time but this time. There is no moment but this moment. "Now" is all there is."
>
> ~ Neale Donald Walsch, Chapter 2, p.28
> *Conversations with God Book 2*

2. Quotes from Other Spiritual Masters

> "What you think of as the past is a memory trace, stored in the mind, of a former Now. When you remember the past, you reactivate a memory trace – and you do so Now. The future is an imagined Now, a projection of the mind. When the future comes, it comes as the Now. When you think about the future, you do it now. Past and future obviously have no reality of their own."
>
> ~ Eckhart Tolle
> *The Power of Now*

> "When you're with people who recognize and own their negative qualities, you never feel judged by them. It's only when people see good and bad, right and wrong, as qualities outside themselves that judgments occur."
>
> ~ Deepak Chopra
> *The Seven Spiritual Laws of Success*

3. Principles & Objectives

Principles:

Given the same set of circumstances, education, background and experiences, any human being has the potential to show unlimited behavior. There is no good or bad. There IS. Everyone acts from his/her own level of consciousness.

Learning Objectives:

A) You will develop the ability to be in present moment awareness.

B) You will learn to accept yourself as perfect the way you are.

4. Exercises

Conversations with God book 2, Chapter 3- Affirmation

"My intention is to experience present moment awareness and accept myself as perfect."

---

1. Introspect about present moment awareness. Create perfection within.

   When you start having anxiety about the past or worry about the future, stop. Bring your attention to the present moment only. For example, If you are working at your desk, listen to the sounds surrounding you. Feel the desk you are working on, its texture. Look through the window and be aware of what is happening outside. If there is no window, look at something and observe what it is made of: its color, scent, shape?

   Answer these questions in repetition. Note your changing answers.
   - Have you done anything outside of the present moment? Do you think you ever will?
   - Have you ever felt anything outside of the present moment? Do you think you ever will?
   - Have you ever experienced anything outside of the present moment? Do you think you ever will?
   - Have you ever thought anything outside of the present moment? Do you think you ever will?

---

2. Turn to a fresh page in your journal.
   - On the left hand side, write down three qualities that you really like about yourself.
   - On the right hand side of your page, name someone you don't appreciate and write down three faults of that person.
   - Draw a circle around both faults and qualities. All these personality traits represent who you are !

3. When you are with someone try consciously to:
   - Make eye contact, smile with your eyes
   - Send caring energy, silently.
   - Practice this often.

When you practice this experiment, the other person will receive, consciously or unconsciously, the respect and care you are sending within. Including your facial expression, tone of voice and your body language will be acknowledged at a very deep level.

4. Working in the mirror can be very deeply moving:
   - Looking directly into your eyes in the mirror.
   - Acknowledge the beauty of your reflection.
   - Smile.
   - Send a very compassionate look to yourself.
   - As you watch yourself, gently caress your arms, kiss your hands
   - Say: "You are so beautiful and talented, and everything is OK."

KEY DEFINITION for Chapter 3:

Present moment awareness: a way of *being* as opposed to something we do. A reliable indicator that we have entered present moment awareness is that our life experience, no matter how it may appear outwardly, is infused inwardly with deeply felt gratitude. This appreciation is not founded on comparison. This is not a gratitude that only blossoms because our life is unfolding exactly how we want it to or because everything feels perfectly easy. It is a gratefulness for the invitation, the journey, and the gift *of life itself*. It is gratitude that requires no reason, nor understanding. Gratitude is the one single marker that we can depend on as an indicator of how present and *in the now* we are in our life experience. If we have no gratitude for being alive, it is because we have strayed from the moment, back into our past or jumping into our future of how we think life is *supposed to* be.

5 – Summary of this chapter lesson:
Try reading these questions and writing your answers in a stream-of-thought, not stopping your writing for 10-15 minutes. See what kind of answers come out.

- Upon self-reflection introspecting about present moment awareness, what did you learn?
- How? Why?
- When you realized that all the personality traits of the person you do not like represent who you are, were you in disbelief? Why? After thinking through about these traits, were you able to finally acknowledge them? Was it a difficult task? Why?
- Working in the mirror: how did it make you feel? Why?

Chapter 4

COLLECTIVE CONSCIOUSNESS

Chapter 4 Summary

All events and experiences in life have the purpose of creating opportunity. And, too, life events are the result of collective consciousness. If you are not pleased with the consciousness of the group you belong to, you have a choice: either you leave the group or you remain in it. There are two ways to use consciousness: peace or violence. We may always choose consciously, in full awareness, choose-to-choose.

"Your world, and the condition it is in, is a reflection of the total, combined consciousness of everyone living there."

~ Neale Donald Walsch, Chapter 4, p.51
Conversations with God Book 2

---

2 – Quotes from Other Spiritual Masters

"The way of peace is based on the same thing that ushered in the age of science: a leap in consciousness. When they witnessed demonstrations of steam engines, electric lights, and vaccines, people adapted to them at the level of their own awareness. The idea of being human could no longer be consistent with reading by candlelight, traveling by horse, suffering through high rates of death in childbirth, short life spans, and the ravages of disease. A leap in collective consciousness took place."

~Deepak Chopra, MD
Peace is the Way

---

3 – Principles & Objectives

Principles:
(Core new ideas for the world, according to Neale Donald Walsch)

I. Large numbers of people in a given area behave simultaneously in similar ways and have similar goals that might be different from what they would do individually.

II. Group behavior differs from mass actions. The latter refers to people behaving similarly on a more global scale, while group behavior refers to people in one place, a more localized community.

III. You cannot know cold unless there is hot. Naming and shedding light on the context and contrasts of this life, enlightens our choice moments.

Learning Objectives:

A) You will know, through a heightened sense of self and living it, your state of consciousness and the world's consciousness.

B) You will know how to seek change in group consciousness if you desire because you are not satisfied with it.

C) You will realize that shifting your local group awareness will shift the world view, because there are no separations.

D) You may see your family traditions, your culture, or you religion in a whole new way after this chapter.

4 – Exercises

Conversations with God book 2, Chapter 4- Affirmation

"My desire is to expand my sense of self; to experience a wide open environment where my intentions will connect to a greater expanded consciousness, leading to miracles, peace and harmony."

---

1. To know your <u>personal state of consciousness is to be</u> the observer of what is happening around you. If your sense of self is not open, it will manifest as very tight and fearful; you will not feel secure. You will feel unprotected and unsafe. Your attitude and outward behavior will be considered aggressive, arrogant, greedy, demanding, and unhappy. However, if your sense of self is open, you will have a sense of freedom and peace, and you will feel unrestricted. Your attitude, in that case, will

manifest as being highly creative, nurturing, humble, sharing, compassionate, and generous.

- Note your attitude every day for two weeks.
- Jot down a few words on your calendar each of these days that describes your general characteristics.
- Discuss with a friend.

2. If you want to be aware of <u>the state of collective consciousness</u>, look at what is happening around the world. If the collective sense of self is closed, its identity will be seen as being focused on profit-making, greedy competition, military conflict, violence, fear and search for economic power.

<u>List Part A</u>

<u>Peaceful Attitudes</u>	Conflict or closed Attitudes

3. <u>Awaken in your Group(s)</u>: If communities, societies or institutions were to express their higher, expanded selves, they would transform their group-culture. More Oneness with the world would develop groups oriented toward cooperation, service, nonviolence, humility, peace and justice. This altered behavior would allow a conscious, more balanced, higher evolved world based on respect for all life. This higher level of respect for life would bring an awareness that love ever-expanding is the ultimate underlying force of the universe, of our worlds.

We have learned powerful lessons from past behavior, such as that of Adolf Hitler. We now have a choice to be role models for the future. It starts with shifting within our own selves. Once we change what is happening within our own world, the world around us will change. We may think that it will just be a drop in the ocean, yet many drops will transcend the actual state of world affairs.

<u>List Part B</u>
Consider discussing your lists above with those people you listed. Know that even a dialogue on these topics shifts and changes everyday life.

KEY DEFINITIONS for Chapter 4:

Collective Consciousness: the shared beliefs and moral attitudes which operate as unifying force(s) within society. This term was used by the French social theorist Emile Durkheim (1858-1917) in his books: *The Division of Labour* (1893), *The Rules of Sociological Method* (1895), *Suicide* (1897), and *The Elementary Forms of Religious Life* (1912).

Collective sense of self: attitude, and thus behavior, of a critical mass of people, societies, communities or institutions which tips history.

5 – Summary of this chapter lesson:

- Collectively, we have learned powerful lessons from past behavior, such as Hitler. Think of other collective lessons we have learned from past behavior. Write down half dozen major events that come to mind.

  1) _____
  2) _____
  3) _____
  4) _____
  5) _____
  6) _____

- This life is about contrasts, if you do not know light, then what is darkness? When we desire something, its opposite also shows-up and then <u>you may choose clearly what you desire !</u>

- We always have a choice to be role models for the future. It starts with changing what is happening within our own selves. Once we shift what is happening within our own world, the world around us will change. We may think that it will just be a drop in the ocean, yet billions of drops together will transcend the actual state of world affairs ripple by ripple.

Chapter 5

TIME

Chapter 5 Summary

Time is part of our imagination because the continuity and solidity of our world exists only in our minds. We are just nervous systems exploring our world through our five senses. At that level of perception, we cannot discern the waves of energy and information of existence. At a subatomic level, as deeply explained in quantum physics, we are all vibrating in and out of existence all the time.

Everything in previous lives, in this life, and in future lives is happening right now. We can transcend from a negative, uncomfortable or traumatic past action to a positive, constructive outcome for the future. This is Karma, life action, choice and change. *It is you who are moving.*

Embracing uncertainty is a blessing and a life-flow that brings the fulfillment of our Divine Selves into ever evolving spiritual beings in human form.

"A true understanding of time allows you to live much more peacefully within your reality of relativity, where time is experienced as a movement, a flow, rather than a constant. It is you who are moving, not time. Time has no movement. There is only One Moment."

~ Neale Donald Walsch, Chapter 5, page 58
Conversations with God Book 2

---

2 – Quotes from Other Spiritual Masters

"Without consciousness acting as an observer and interpreter, everything would exist only as pure potential."

Deepak Chopra
The Spontaneous Fulfillment of Desires

> "If I burn myself on a hot stove, that fraction of a second seems like eternity. But if I'm with a beautiful woman, even eternity seems like one second. It's gone in a moment. It's never enough."
>
> ~ Albert Einstein

3 – Principles & Objectives

Principles:

I. The experience of time is subjective, a peaceful flow, or not.

II. When you pay attention to your inner self, versus paying attention to your earthly experiences according to Neale, Ayurveda and a host of other leaders' works, you will allow your inner spirit to be the non judging observer of the oneness of all.

Learning Objectives:

A) You will discover how to change your perception of time.

B) You will be able to break the barrier of time and reach the nonchanging factor (of you and the All) that is always present.

4 – Exercises

Conversations with God book 2, Chapter 5- Affirmation

"All events of my life that I would usually consider the future may be capable of influencing some events of my past."

1. Each time you do something that you really enjoy, like listening to wonderful music, playing a game, feel the beauty of nature around you or falling in love, Stop. Feel. Enjoy. Observe how time flies by when you are immersing in what you love.

2. Each time you don't like doing something, be aware of how long it seems to go through time. Take notes in your journal. How is time going for you?

3. As you remember life events up to now, ask:
   - Who is really remembering or witnessing?
     You have lived experiences as a child, a teenager, an adult, and a changed adult. Yet the "person" witnessing all of your roles is the same, never-changing spirit.

   - Share this experience with someone you trust and compare feelings about it. Collaborative sharing allows you to re-discover and appreciate "who you really are": pure unbounded consciousness.

4. Another experience of time: If you are always running around, your nervous system will speed up. Mentally, set a time and fully allow yourself to *have time*, once daily for a week. Note if your system is calmer or has slowed down.

KEY DEFINITIONS for Chapter 5:

Albert Einstein: best known for his theory of relativity and specifically mass–energy equivalence, $E = mc^2$. Einstein received the 1921 Nobel Prize in Physics "for his services to Theoretical Physics, and especially for his discovery of the law of the photoelectric effect."

Quantum physics: a branch of science that deals with discrete, indivisible units of energy called quanta. There are five main ideas represented in Quantum Theory:

1. Energy is not continuous, it comes in small and discrete units.
2. The elementary particles behave both like particles *and* like waves.
3. The movement of these particles is inherently random.
4. It is *physically impossible* to know both the position and the momentum of a particle at the same time. The more precisely one is known, the less precise the measurement of the other is.
5. The atomic world is *nothing* like the world we live in.

At a glance, this may seem like just another strange or complex theory, yet quantum physics holds the fundamental nature of the universe. It describes the nature of the universe as being much different then the world we *physically see*. As Niels Bohr said, "Anyone who is not shocked by quantum theory has not understood it."

Karma = Action: action leads to memories, which leads to desires, which create action again. You drink a glass of milk. This is the action of drinking. The taste of milk develops a memory. That memory creates a desire to either drink more milk or never drink milk again. The action of drinking milk or not, at a later date, is the result of a choice you made, i.e. ACTION.

Ayurveda: an ancient medicine system of health care. "Ayurveda" roughly translates as the "knowledge of life." Life is defined as the "combination of the body, sense organs, mind and soul, the factor responsible for preventing decay and death, which sustains the body over time, and guides the processes of rebirth". Ayurveda protects "ayus," by healthy living practices and therapeutic measures that promote physical, mental, social and spiritual harmony. Ayurveda is one of the few traditional systems that contains sophisticated medicine for the integration of mind/body/soul.

5 – Summary of this chapter lesson:

- Self-reflect and make an assessment about what you learned in this chapter. Ask self:
  - What did you find out about time?
  - What about your relationship to time?
  - How can you consciously change time for self?
  - How is your health affected by your attitude about time?

- When sharing the experience of remembering your life events up to now with someone ask:
  - What issues and topics came up for you?
  - For both of you?
  - Each of you experiences something when together, describe in details to one another.

Chapter 6

SPACE

Chapter 6 Summary

What we perceive as *objects are in reality empty space.* Yet when we touch an object, we feel solidity ! This is our interpretation of the physical domain, the field of molecules. We are programmed to see and feel objects through our five senses. Our nervous system is the instrument of that perception. So it is only in our consciousness that our limited senses create a solid world.

If we were small enough, we could navigate at the quantum level, and we could see that everything we think is solid, is, in fact, blinking in and out of a limitless void at the speed of light. And through pure potentiality and choice, we can take quantum leaps of creativity to enhance our lives.

We all – men and women – have the infinite possibility to express our feminine and masculine sides.

"Actually, what you call matter is mostly space. All "solid" objects are 2 percent solid "matter" and 98 percent "air" !

~Neale Donald Walsch
Conversations with God Book 2, p.69

---

2 – Quotes from Other Spiritual Masters

"Space, in Ayurvedic terms, is the emptiness in which unlimited potential resides. In this sense, space can be described as the outermost manifestation of the mind, which also encompasses infinite possibilities. Ayurveda teaches that space is the field of unlimited potential from which consciousness creates the material universe."

~ David Simon, MD
Wisdom of Healing

---

3 – Principles & Objectives

Principles:
(Core new ideas for the world, according to Neale Donald Walsch)

I. In our lives, we experience the past in our memory and the future in our imagination.

II. Everything happens simultaneously. At the level of spirituality, the past, the future and all the different possibilities of life exist at the same time.

Learning Objectives:

A) You will develop the intention to think and act with flexibility.
B) You will observe a system to take creativity leaps.

4 – Exercises

> ***Conversations with God book 2**, Chapter 6- Affirmation*
>
> **"My intention is to think and act with flexibility to be able to take quantum leaps of creativity."**

1. It is easy to get into habits and repeat old patterns that are not serving you. This is why it is so important to practice new ways of thinking and acting. Decide to break some habits. Make a list of things you do on regular basis and find other ways of doing them.

   <u>What I Do</u>   <u>How I Can Do this Differently</u>

   Opinions about Someone
   Opinion about Something
   Kinds of music
   Clothing types
   When I regularly awaken
   Exercise?
   Types of books

2. Do this for two weeks, see what happens and write the effects in your journal.

3. To learn how to think out of the ordinary is to first dream the impossible, or what seems impossible from our own perspective. Even if you don't know how your dream will materialize, just believe. Dream big ! Right here, this is a leap. You jump from one way of thinking to a new one with nothing in

between. We have unlimited creative power that we can use to face and solve any situation in our lives.

Take one dream and...
- Write down your intentions in clear present tense.
- Evaluate the challenges you will be facing.
- Speak with friends and family.
- Do some research on the internet, in books or go to seminars.
- Analyze everything, based on the information that you have collected, to access a complete new understanding of the situation.
- Let it seat for a while. Processing takes time.
- Use a meditation technique* to allow your mind to open up and slow down to let something to show up in a way that you have not imagined before.

Reflection:
- How has your perception of the dream shifted?
- This is a leap of creativity.
- Consider now that *nothing* will stop you in solving your intention !
- You can experience different ways of living. You can be ready to be pro- active, because you know what needs to be done to create your dream.
- Look now that challenges in your life will become an opportunity for new solutions into fresh dreams.

*Easy beginner's meditation technique:

1. Sit comfortably and close your eyes.
2. Wait a few seconds.
3. Start to pay attention to your breath.
4. Don't force or concentrate.
5. As you listen to your breath, you may notice that you attention has drifted away from your breath to other thoughts in your mind, a noise around you, or a sensation in your body. When you realize that your attention has drifted away from your breath, bring it back to your breath.
6. Practice meditation for 15-30 minutes.
7. Always take a few minutes to come out of meditation before going back to activity.

KEY DEFINITIONS for Chapter 6:

Consciousness: Being aware and awake to our *Pure Potentiality*

Quantum leap: a leap from A to C, without passing through any of the points between A and C. Imagine that you board an airplane in Paris and just as you take your seat the plane instantly transports you to your New York destination. You just made a quantum leap. The plane didn't pass through any point between Paris and New York in this imagining.

5 – Summary and Extension of this chapter lesson:

Gentle Reminder: use your notebook and sketchbooks for these chapter summary questions and answers. They may be familiar questions, yet after each chapter you have grown and shifted. You are asked to consider how and why to further evolve you !

- When practicing new ways of thinking and acting, have you been able to observe how you felt in your mind and in your body? What were your observations?

- If observation seems a challenge, try watching yourself on your own life stage. Note your feelings as you do this.

- To take quantum leaps of creativity, it is important to really think out of your own ordinary, routine, daily thought processes. It has been said that the definition of insanity is to do the same thing over and over again, expecting a different outcome. Change something and note how you do during this change. Write or sketch these details.

- When dreaming the impossible, what happens to you inside?
    - Does dreaming create a new level of energy?
    - Do you know that you are on the right track to fulfill your dream?
    - Describe or sketch these answers.

Chapter 7

SEXUALITY

Chapter 7 Summary

It is OK to love sex, but more than that, to love yourself. Sex is a celebration of love.

In Tantra, masturbation is widely encouraged as a way to share and give pleasure to others for joyful union of mind, body and spirit.

Having sex is not only for making babies. Sexual expression is part of human nature. It is part of the energy flow of life. We are all sending vibes, and these vibes can be felt all the time everywhere.

Neale:
"Why did you create two sexes? Was this the only way you could figure for us to recreate ? How should we deal with this incredible experience called sexuality?"

God:
"Not with shame, that's for sure. And not with guilt, and not with fear. For shame is not virtue, and guilt is not goodness, and fear is not honor......And, obviously, not with ideas of control or power or domination, for these have nothing to do with Love."

~ Neale Donald Walsch
Conversation with God Book 2, page 74

---

2 – Quotes from Other Spiritual Masters

"It is not enough to teach children in school the mechanics of sexuality. We need on a very deep level to allow children to remember that their bodies, genitals, and sexuality are something to rejoice about."

~ Louise Hay
You can Heal your Life

---

3 – Principles & Objectives

Principles:

I. Love yourself. Do everything for your highest good and everyone else's highest good.

II. The teachings of Tantra can enhance our embracing of life and allow diving transcending from any experience into ecstatic experiences.

III. The Law of Attraction: energy is felt by both men and women and, when understood, can lead to increased pleasure.

Learning Objectives:

A) You will learn how to transform your feelings and beliefs about sexuality into a newfound freedom.

B) You will open your mind about how sex can enter your life in a new way.

C) You will learn how to understand and use energy as a place of Divine Union.

4 – Exercises

> ***Conversations with God book 2**, Chapter 7- Affirmation*
>
> **"To wake up my body, slow down my mind and free my spirit will allow me to reach other levels of consciousness, leading me to ecstasy."**

1. In your journal, write down all the things you feel and believe about sex.
   - What did you learn from your parents about your body? Was it beautiful or something to hide?
   - At school, what did you learn from your teacher about sex?
   - In your religion or culture, was sex considered a negative, a sin that deserved punishment?
   - May be your parents gave a nickname to your genitals?
   - Have you been hurt sexually when you were a child?
   - Do you feel ashamed of your body?
   - Are you afraid to tell or show your partner what feels good to you?

2. Now set up a date with yourself. Take a whole day.
   STEP 1 – TREAT YOURSELF AT HOME
   Make sure your bathroom is warm enough, because you will be nude for an hour or so.
   - Start by taking a sensual bath. Set out candles and burn some incense of your choice. Put on some nice, relaxing music. Add oils or bubbles

in your bath, and make it the right temperature for you. Use your favorite fragrance. Undress and hold or fold your clothes with care. Slowly let yourself sink down into the water. Feel the water caressing each part of your body. After 15 minutes of joy in your bath, get out of the bath and dry yourself off gently. Take good care

- Look for things you like about your body. Get a hand mirror and go to your full length mirror. Look at every inch of your body and find some area where you can find something to like. It can be the color or the sweetness of your skin, the curve of your hip or the beauty of your hands. Don't forget to examine your sexual organs with your hand mirror and observe the different color and skin tissue and your hair growth. Using your full length mirror, try different positions that make you the most attractive. Play with your eyes and your smile. With your arms, hug yourself with tenderness and say to yourself, looking into your eyes: "I love you !"

- Touching yourself. Lie down on your bed and with your hands, start drawing circles on the inside of your forearm. Make a note of what you like: do you prefer light or heavier pressure? Do you like it fast or slower? Now take a small amount of your massage body oil. Warm it up in your hands and start making circles again inside of your forearm. Start applying your body oil on both sides of your neck, on your shoulders, around your eyes, on your ears, all parts of your face, including your lower lip and upper lip. Move on to your chest and nipples, your stomach, your legs, your feet and your toes. Next, apply more body oil directly on your genitals and start to slowly explore by touching yourself, noticing which particular places are the most sensitive.

STEP 2 – EXPLORING YOURSELF

- Energy centers. Tantra recognizes seven energy centers in the body. These energy centers are know as Chakras in Sanskrit. Using the power of your intention, you can clear the toxins that limit the full expression of your prana (Sanskrit word for life force):

- Sit down in a comfortable position, eyes closed, shoulders relaxed, hands on your lap, palms up.

- Start to bring your attention to the base of the spine (1st chakra), take a deep breath and release the sound LAM as if it was coming from that 1st chakra, allowing the sound to raise your energy level. Keep the sound going as long as your exhalation allows it.

- Move up to your sexual organs, with the sound VAM, the same way you did for the 1st one.

- To the solar plexus with the sound RAM,

- To the heart with the sound YUM,

- To the throat with the sound HUM,

- To the forehead with the sound SHAM,

- To the crown of the head with the sound AUM.

KEY DEFINITIONS for Chapter 7:

Tantra: Asian system of beliefs and practices which, working from the principle that the universe we experience is nothing other than the concrete manifestation of the divine energy of the Godhead that creates and maintains that universe, seeks through rituals and practices to appropriate and channel that energy, within the human connections, in creative and growing ways.

Chakras: vortices or centers of subtle and sometimes not-so-subtle energies, moving in a spinning motion. If the energy within the chakra system is clear and flowing freely, you will experience happiness and peaceful flow in your life, as well as an increased sexual energy. The process of clearing the energy blocks within the chakra system takes determination and trust.

Sanskrit: an ancient Indo-European classical language of India.

Prana: Sanskrit word that refers to a vital, life-sustaining force of living beings and vital energy in natural processes of the universe. Prana is a central concept in Ayurveda and Yoga where it is believed to flow through a network of fine subtle channels called nadis in the center of the human body.

5 – Summary of this chapter lesson:
Try changing the way you self-reflect here. Draw if you have been writing. Record or film if you've been writing. Listen to yourself in newfound ways.
Read the statements below and bring into form answers and whole thoughts that are right for you, especially after the discoveries in the chapter:

- Many of us grew up thinking that sex is dirty, sex is a sin or that you have to be a certain way, with only a certain person or even be married to have sex. Some also believe that sex is only to procreate. Sometimes, we feel that our bodies are not beautiful enough or we don't dare ask for what we want, especially sexually.
- We have a tendency to look at the parts of our body that we don't like. This time, you made a quantum leap to be a person who is committed to have more and more pleasure in your life.
- In the experience of touching yourself with body oil, how did it feel? Did it feel differently from using dry hands?
- The more you learn about what feels good for you, the more you will know how good it feels for your partner and the less inhibition you will have about the whole process of making love, including asking your partner whether or not it feels good and whether your partner needs more or less of something.
- Continue this chapter in your own way. Try to allow this information to grow in your daily life, for you have shifted. How have you shifted? Comment on this. Share with a partner or friend what you are learning…

Chapter 8

HIGHER STATES OF CONSCIOUSNESS

Chapter 8 Summary

Any behavior is acceptable in life as a whole, or in sexuality, as long as there is mutual consent among the people involved. This statement needs to be said because, when we look back on past generations – across the world – and when we don't teach our children about sexuality, we build a community ashamed of our body parts and we collectively experience lives with inhibitions and taboos.

In societies where sexual openness is promoted, crimes of passion, rape and prostitution are almost nonexistent. Different positions, unusual or kinky sex, loveless, consenting sex is not wrong. God does not have any judgment about gay sex. People decide for themselves how their physical, spiritual, mental, and emotional growth evolves. When you put yourself first, it is loving, self awareness; it is not selfishness.

We are three-part beings: Body, Mind and Spirit. Getting to higher states of consciousness can bring balance to our lives. And if many spiritual teachers espouse complete abstinence from sex, it is because they don't believe that they can find balance. Enlightenment and growth allow you not to have compulsive behavior about sex or anything else in life.

When someone else dictates what is appropriate for society, it is very limiting for human behavior. Propriety is not related to "rightness" or wrongness," your personal priorities are your choices.

As for propriety, that single word and the behavioral concept behind it have done more to inhibit men's and women's greatest joys than any other human construction – except the idea that God is punitive – which finished the job.

~ Neale Donald Walsch
Conversations with God Book 2, p. 95

---

2 – Quotes from Other Spiritual Masters

"In Cosmic Consciousness, we experience miracles. In Divine Consciousness, we create miracles. In Unified Consciousness, there is no more need for miracles, for everything is perceived as miraculous."

~ Deepak Chopra, MD
Primordial Sound Meditation

3 – Principles & Objectives

Principles:

I. We are three part-beings: Body, Mind and Spirit.

II. Adi Shankara, an influential teacher and leader in philosophy of yoga and Veda in the ninth century, described these three parts as Layers of Life:

   1- The Body: the physical part with our personal body, our energy and our environment.
   2- The Subtle part: the Mind, the Intellect and the Ego.
   3- The Spirit part: the Soul, the domain of Archetypes, and the Universal domain.

III. We limit our experiences to three levels of consciousness: sleeping, dreaming and living. Deepak Chopra describes higher levels of consciousness:

   1. Pure awareness level: silence between the thoughts found in meditation practice.

   2. Witnessing level: we observe ourselves in different situations of our lives from spirit, which is part of who we really are.

   3. Divine level: we are all interconnected with everything else in creation.

   4. Unified level: the full expression of yoga, the unification of individuality with universality.

Learning Objectives:

A) Through meditation, you will find balance.
B) Quieting your inner commotion and your actions will allow more creative power.
C) Your purpose to find peace, health and love will be satisfied.

4 – Exercises

***Conversations with God book 2*, Chapter 8- Affirmation**

"I will approach my life in a thoughtful and intelligent manner by making a commitment to meditation as a way to improve in my physical, mental, emotional, and spiritual domains."

---

1. Evaluate how your days are organized. See how you might find more balance.

   a) Try regular meditation practice into your daily activities.
   b) It is recommended, for maximum benefits, that you meditate 30 minutes twice daily.
   c) Keep it up ! Try a variety of meditation.

2. People benefit from different kinds of meditations and relaxation techniques. It is important that your inner calming tools be comfortable. Here are some examples of meditations techniques:

   - Chanting meditation
   - Healing meditation, energy, etc.
   - Breathing meditation
   - Prayer meditation: reading a prayer or reflecting on any of their words.
   - Music meditation
   - Read a beloved meditation aloud as you record yourself; play your voice back for a special healing, quieting of self.

3. Establishing a good foundation of meditation techniques will allow you to go beyond the mind and re-connect with your spirit. And this is the same spirit that flows with everything in creation. You could go on line and check these two powerful meditation techniques:

   Transcendental meditation: www.tm.org
   Primordial Sound meditation: www.chopra.com

4. Meditation is like coming home to Who We Really Are. There is nothing scary about it, though it may seem new and unusual for you. When we meditate, we can develop a very secure, wonderful place to be.

The process is multi-fold. It allows us to:
   - melt-away stress
   - slow your heart-rate
   - travel and flow with life more easily
   - nurture self in a ritual, that eventually teaches how to calm self at any time.

We are on a spiritual journey in physical bodies to re-discover Who We Really Are. "Rediscover" because we already know, but we have forgotten due to so many of our earthly experiences.

KEY DEFINITIONS for Chapter 8:

Propriety: conformity to established standards of proper behavior or manners.

Vedas: (Sanskrit for "knowledge") are a large corpus of texts originating in Ancient India. They form the oldest layer of Sanskrit literature and the oldest sacred texts of Hinduism.

Universal domain: Pure potentiality, infinite possibilities.

5 – Summary and Extension of this chapter lesson:

- When practicing your meditation, what have you learned about yourself by staying quiet, in silence?
- Did you experience a lot of thoughts?
- Did you fall asleep?
- Did you feel bliss?
- Whatever happened was perfect because this is what was supposed to happen. Don't worry, keep practicing, you will get the benefits. More benefits come as you practice.

Chapter 9

EDUCATION

"Wisdom is knowledge applied."

Chapter 9 Summary

Education is about wisdom. It is not about *just facts, knowledge, nor relearning the same things from generation to generation.* The new spirituality difference is that wisdom is *knowledge applied and experienced* for ourselves. We teach our children about math, geography, history, languages, physics, and often we are not teaching them how to think -- how to unveil their own truths. Parents, teachers and many adults feel threatened by the concept of wisdom versus knowledge because the fear is that with such education, children might abandon their parent's way of life, or at least reframe it and not do exactly as those before them. In many current societies, we have not taught our children that they are spiritual beings in a body *having their own experiences and that their experiences are valid.*

Is this non-teaching working for our human species?

History, *taught to the children as facts of life,* is just replication of the facts, not teaching or modeling evolving and changing reality. Young people are begging their parents and teachers to stop doing what the collective world has been and still is doing.

Are we hearing? Are we even listening?

If denied, if not listened to, young people are going elsewhere to feel accepted, to feel heard. As a result, young people join gangs looking to be accepted and heard. They are killing each other and themselves as a way of life. And at a staggering rate, suicide has risen. Suicide statistics are not just statistics, they are not numbers but sad realities of children dropping out of life.

In a more evolved education, a more evolved society with higher evolved beings (HEBs) we treat our young people as precious spirits housed in human bodies – *with equal souls to adults.* Yes, equal souls ! We can bring out and unveil *from them* what really is true and natural for them; we can draw from the inside, out, their 'divine spark' of God in new ways of education !

A fresh, free, 21st century new spirituality curriculum could be built around three core concepts:

- Awareness

- Honesty

- Responsibility

We *can still* teach our children our past data, while also teaching to analyze those facts anew. We *can ask and listen* to our young for their perspectives and their solutions, rather than simply reiterating history and facts given as 'ultimate truths' to live again and again, reliving the same old, same old mistakes…

"Most of the human race has decided that the meaning and the purpose and the function of education is to pass on knowledge; that to educate someone is to give them knowledge – generally, the accumulated knowledge of one's particular family, clan, tribe, society, nation, and world. Yet, education has very little to do with knowledge."

~ Neale Donald Walsch
Conversations with God Book 2, p. 110

2 – Quotes from Other Spiritual Masters

"I had always given the first place to the culture of the heart or the building of character and as I felt confident that moral training could be given to all alike, no matter how different their ages and their upbringing, I decided to live amongst them all the twenty-four hours of the day as their father. I regarded character building as the proper foundation for their education and, if the foundation was firmly laid, I was sure that the children could learn all the other things themselves or with the assistance of friends."

~ Gandhi

3 – Principles & Objectives

Principles:

Let us teach our young children practical, self-evolutional courses such as:

- Understanding Power
- Peaceful Conflict Resolution
- Elements of Loving Relationships
- Personhood and Self Creation
- Body, Mind and Spirit: How They Function
- Engaging Creativity
- Celebrating Self, Valuing Others
- Joyous Sexual Expression
- Fairness
- Tolerance
- Diversities and Similarities
- Ethical Economics
- Creative Consciousness and Mind Power
- Awareness and Wakefulness
- Honesty and Responsibility
- Visibility and Transparency
- Science and Spirituality

(The School of the New Spirituality is bringing these topics into the world through programs, services and interactive materials such as this guidebook.)

Learning Objectives:

A) You will learn about the different learning environs which are already approaching a new type of curriculum.

B) You will now consider treating children with the respect an honor befitting equal souls to ourselves.

4 – Exercises

Conversations with God book 2, **Chapter 9- Affirmations**

"My desire is to be part of our next generation's growth. I will make conscious choices about my children's education."

"Wisdom is knowledge applied."

"Namaste means: The Divine in me, sees the Divine in you."

---

1. In your journal make a list of your children's strengths and lesser strengths. Think about the opportunity to provide support for them in each of these areas, especially in the areas where they excel. Play with them in their passions, their loves. If they like what they do, they will be willing to improve even more. Passions build terrific life purposes and create lifelong motivation to learn.

Children in My Life		
Name	Strengths	Lesser Strengths

2. Take time to search for the best options for the children in your life. Consider nieces, nephews or friends' children, if you do not have your own. Study the learning model charts in this chapter. Search on the web using the information provided following the charts. Open your mind to different education systems, ways of learning and different ways to touch the children who touch your life. You are affecting your future through the children. You do make a significant difference, if you choose.

3. Ask your child:

   a) What do you think and feel are your strengths, loves, and skills?
   b) "What role do you wish to play now or in your future?"
   c) "Who do you need to support you in your next vision for yourself?"
   d) Date and note in detail the child's answers.
   e) Continue this sharing by welcoming drawing or sketching with your child about these very important questions.
   f) Ask again every six months or so. It is a joy to see the evolution of these ideas ! And the very act of asking means you do not have to have the answers. This activity is a discovery journey *for you and the child.*

4. Now consider the learning models in the world and how your new spirituality study is creating different learning for you and your family. Note very specifically in your journal or the pages at the back of this guidebook, what you feel and think after reading the charts to follow and tomorrow's education.

SNS – Alternative Learning Models Comparison Chart – seeing new spirituality approaches next to other learning systems

MODEL	SNS New Spirituality Learning Model	Montessori	Summerhill	Sudbury Valley "democratic" models	Waldorf	Ananda	Reggio Emilia	Homeschool & Unschooling
FOUNDED	1997 (concept) 2000 1st new spirituality school Ashland, Oregon. 3 more in USA & South Africa	1907 Italy	1921 England	1963 Boston, Massachusetts	1919 Germany	1917 India 1968 California	1940s Italy	1,000s of years ago; resurgence in 1980s
PHILO-SOPHICAL UNDER-PINNINGS	N.D. Walsch's philosophy as set forth in his books, *Conversations with God*, and transformational perspectives about education Reflected in "HeartLight Learning Model" in the SNS Manual on line	Maria Montessori's pediatric medical research	A.S. Neill's philosophy as set forth in his book: *Summerhill: A Radical Approach to Child Rearing*	Hanna & Daniel Greenberg and Mimsy Sadofsky, inspired and influenced by A.S. Neill's Summerhill and Greenberg's book, *Free at Last*. "It takes a village to raise a child." ~ African proverb	Rudolf Steiner's philosophy of anthroposophy (from anthroposophy meaning humanity and Sophia meaning wisdom)	Based on the philosophical principles of Paramahansa Yogananda and his disciple J. Donald Walters	Began after the post-WWII devastation of the town of Reggio Emilia, Italy; 12% of the town budget is committed to quality early childhood education thru age 6. Upper-ages Reggio are developing worldwide	The home is the best environment for learning. "Real learning is a process of discovery…we must create the kinds of conditions in which discoveries are made…time, freedom, and a lack of pressure." ~ John Holt
MODEL	SNS New Spirituality	Montessori	Summerhill	Sudbury Valley "democratic" models	Waldorf	Ananda	Reggio Emilia	Homeschool & Unschooling

MODEL	SNS New Spirituality Learning Model	Montessori	Summerhill	Sudbury Valley "democratic" models	Waldorf	Ananda	Reggio Emilia	Homeschool & Unschooling
PHILOSOPHY IN A NUTSHELL	Purpose is to empower everyone (students and staff) to discover who they really are as spiritual beings, and to develop and express their full potential in real-life performance roles. Reconnecting with GOD in new ways… "Learning is when the heart, mind and soul come together and agree what is so." ~ N.D. Walsch	"We are here to offer to this life the means necessary for the development, and having done that we must await this development with respect." ~ M. Montessori, MD Credo: "Help me to do it myself."	"Education should be a preparation for life." ~ A.S. Neill. "All the child needs is the three R's; the rest should be tools and clay and sports and theater and paint and freedom." ~ A.S. Neill. Summerhill is a boarding school in England in which all lessons are optional	"Central to the school is the idea that children learn judgment by coping with real-world problems….the only way children can become responsible citizens is to BE responsible for their own welfare, their own education, and their own destiny." ~ Free at Last	"Anthroposophy does not only want to impart knowledge, it seeks to awaken life." ~ R. Steiner. Credo: Protection of childhood by creating a safe school environment where imagination, play (a child's work) and socialization are nurtured	"A growing child needs to learn how to live in this world, and not merely how to find a job. He or she needs to know how to live wisely, happily, and successfully according to deep inner needs." ~ J.D. Walters	Learning occurs in context thru listening, valuing, developing, displaying, and learning with children. Physical environment is interesting, aesthetically pleasing, open to the community, and interactive	Learning is organic, coming out of life and personal interests. Parents homeschool for varied reasons including religious preference, underperforming public schools, or to accommodate child's learning style or a philosophical approach different from local schools
MODEL	SNS New Spirituality	Montessori	Summerhill	Sudbury Valley "democratic" models	Waldorf	Ananda	Reggio Emilia	Homeschool & Unschooling

MODEL	SNS New Spirituality Learning Model	Montessori	Summerhill	Sudbury Valley "democratic" models	Waldorf	Ananda	Reggio Emilia	Homeschool & Unschooling
DIVING DEEPER INTO THE PHILO-SOPHY	Awareness, Honesty, Responsibility; Bringing God into the learning conversation in new ways; Intentions are to: create a community of learning that is conscious, creative, collaborative, competent, compassionate. Essence: drawing from the inside of a child out. Rather than feeding info into the youth. SNS is supporting a Civil Rights movement of the Child's SOUL; all souls are equal... Honor and advance everyone's capacity for leading self-directed, self-assessing, self-renewing lives. Develop students' intellectual, intuitive, interpersonal, emotional, and performance capabilities	Child has an absorbent mind ready to soak up knowledge and experiences. Learning experiences are arranged in sequential fashion: keep supplying ever-more-challenging intellectual tasks and the child will be educated. Teacher is distinguished organizer and observer who respects students' personal styles	Child's well-being is more important than academic development. Teachers are facilitators. Learning experiences are not ordered; child chooses the order of learning experiences out of interest and curiosity. "...all outside compulsion is wrong, ...inner compulsion is the only value." ~ A.S. Neill	Child is ultimately responsible for his own education. Teachers are facilitators. Staff (by being attentive, caring and non-coercive) give children the courage and impetus to listen to their own inner selves. Learning experiences are not ordered; child chooses the order as at Summerhill	Emphasis on enhancing child's creative thinking, imagination, and world of fantasy. No early thrust into intellectualism. It unfolds slowly as the child moves from one developmental stage to the next. Seeks to transform humanity and the world thru inherent wisdom	"...strives to provide real direction for constructive change in schools, home, and society." ~ Education for Life Foundation. "...a wonderful alternative for parents who are looking not only for intellectual development, but also development of heart qualities"	Simultaneous faith in children, parents, and teachers to contribute in meaningful ways to the choice of school experiences. Focus on children's symbolic languages (including art, dramatic play, & writing) in context of a project-based curriculum, and on visual documentation of development	Parent is ultimately responsible for the child's education
MODEL	SNS New Spirituality	Montessori	Summerhill	Sudbury Valley "democratic" models	Waldorf	Ananda	Reggio Emilia	Homeschool & Unschooling

MODEL	SNS New Spirituality Learning Model	Montessori	Summerhill	Sudbury Valley "democratic" models	Waldorf	Ananda	Reggio Emilia	Homeschool & Unschooling
CURRICULUM	Environment is learner-centered and often collaborative. Learners explore individual interests and learn universal themes, concepts, and life skills (including technology, the arts, and "the three R's") in the context of their own passions. Learners identify, explore, and develop their unique combinations of talents and interests and express those gifts fully in their lives. Curriculum vehicles include dream and interest files, project plans, student-teacher contracts with clear timeframes and goals	Thru age 4: sensory experiences, language development, coordination and movement, time and space, sequence, truth and reality. Ages 4-6: continuation & refinement of the above, writing, tactile sense, reading. Age 6 up: traditional subjects in experiential classroom structure plus: music, art, cooking, languages. Traditional academic material in upper grades in open class format	Classes are optional, but are offered in English and other languages, math, history, science, geography, art, pottery, sports, woodworking, drama. Democratic process learned thru daily involvement in it	No standard offerings; student asks for lessons (private or group) on specific skills. Student discovers own path and defends her own way at school meetings. TV, videogames, and music room unlimited on a signup basis; TV used for specific real world events. Certification for use of equipment such as dark room and computers. Democratic process learned thru daily involvement in it	Waldorf schools predetermine all curriculum; education seen as an ascending spiral. All students participate in all basic subjects regardless of their special aptitudes. Day begins with a long, uninterrupted lesson on a single subject and focus followed by recitation, movement, concentration and review. Afternoons spent in eurhythmy (artistically guided movement to music and speech, handwork, art, or gym)	K-6: art, self-understanding; balance of body, mind and heart; harmony with others and nature; expansive spirit, development of positive attitudes and intuition. High school: character training; traditional academic skills taught from a perspective of personal growth; spiritual development; yoga, meditation and service to others; Italian; the arts; adventure; personal worth and self-confidence. Integrated technology	Thru age 6: same as Montessori. Age 6 up: traditional subjects in experiential classroom structure, plus: music, art, and foreign language. Technology is explored then integrated into activities when appropriate	Frequently echoes public schools using traditional curriculum and school texts. Frequent use of computer technology and/or workbooks. Additional curriculum may focus on religious teachings and texts, the arts, or on home-based skills and handicrafts such as cooking and sewing
MODEL	SNS New Spirituality	Montessori	Summerhill	Sudbury Valley "democratic" models	Waldorf	Ananda	Reggio Emilia	Homeschool & Unschooling

MODEL	SNS New Spirituality Learning Model	Montessori	Summerhill	Sudbury Valley "democratic" models	Waldorf	Ananda	Reggio Emilia	Homeschool & Unschooling
METHODS	* Teacher guides work with students and parents to develop individual learning plans, set goals, and assess outcomes * As lead learners, adults facilitate acquisition of knowledge by providing resources and materials * Learning environment intentionally set up to encourage self-awareness, self-discovery and conscious intellectual * Concepts and skills may be taught thru carefully structured mini-lessons and planned experiences	* Teacher is detached observer * Classroom set up w/ Montessori researched real-life activities; use of Montessori certified equipment & tools * Environment manipulated for the exercise of the child's free interest * Learning paced at child's development levels * Discovery and awareness fostered through role modeling * Children engage in real-life house-keeping responsibilities	* Staff facilitates classes and learning * Students initiate their own learning activities and environments; they may ask for (or attend) specific lessons (private or group) on student selected topics	* Staff facilitates classes and learning * Play considered an active learning experience; games numerous and spontaneous * Oral communication is center of learning environment * Upon request, community experts share knowledge * Student's time for inner concentration is protected; quiet room (with sign-up for periods of time) is respected	* Environment arranged so that child has an underlying sense of order that helps her to feel secure	* Individualized approach * Creative expression through art * Boys and girls attend separate classes	* Project approach to learning; projects (developed from mutual interests of student and teacher) include real-life problem-solving, creative thinking, and exploration * Spontaneous play supported and used as basis for emergent lessons	* Parents often team teach or build activities in concert with other homeschoolers * Field trips often provide a base or follow-up for learning * Job-shadowing and other experiential forms of learning
MODEL	SNS New Spirituality	Montessori	Summerhill	Sudbury Valley "democratic" models	Waldorf	Ananda	Reggio Emilia	Homeschool & Unschooling

MODEL	SNS New Spirituality Learning Model	Montessori	Summerhill	Sudbury Valley "democratic" models	Waldorf	Ananda	Reggio Emilia	Homeschool & Unschooling
ASSESSMENT	**Assessment is embedded in finished products, projects, and performances. Regular learner-led family conferences are scheduled. Learners share portfolios and their progress on long-term projects. Adults focus on learning about the child in order to provide guidance and structure. Next goals and development are based on previous learning. Standardized tests are used when necessary to reach goals**	Grade-level standards of learning are assessed by teacher before student may move to next level	Standard English school leaving exams optional, not compulsory. Students wishing to go to college may, by mutual agreement with teacher, take "A" (advanced) level exams versus "O" (ordinary) levels. "Tests are for fun – for promotion of thought and unseriousness." ~ A.S. Neill	No grade levels. Students may opt for testing any time for self discovery (optional). A high school certificate application is defended by student & voted for approval by school assembly / meeting. Student may choose SAT instruction from book or teacher & take test for college. Some students attend college by entrance interview in lieu of SAT	Traditional study and testing with life immersion experiences	A variety of standard and school generated testing. Standardized grade-level testing may be used	Emphasis on visual and intrinsic documentation of child's development. Assessment based on developmental level, not age, and includes narrative reports, anecdotal notes, photos, and other evidence of child's development. Teachers' journals are planning guides for future lessons	Life performance serves as "tests." Standardized testing may be required by local school districts. Parents may make their own traditional chapter tests. Diplomas may be available to homeschoolers connected with a private school network
MODEL	SNS New Spirituality	Montessori	Summerhill	Sudbury Valley "democratic" models	Waldorf	Ananda	Reggio Emilia	Homeschool & Unschooling

MODEL	SNS New Spirituality Learning Model	Montessori	Summerhill	Sudbury Valley "democratic" models	Waldorf	Ananda	Reggio Emilia	Homeschool & Unschooling
GOVERNANCE	What works? What doesn't? Questions with discoveries to allow youth to find own answers. Holistic Living CoreConcepts: Functionality, Adaptability, Sustainability; Values are stressed over rules. Daily class meetings co-develop together learning culture of listening, drawing from within, out, caring and respect, grounded in the sense and discussion of GOD. Teacher-guides help students craft rules as needed in order to ensure a safe environment conducive to learning. Group consent circles replace voting as a decision-making tool	Schools are independently owned with the choice of affiliating with USA or International Montessori by yearly fees, the hiring of certified teachers who receive a full year of training at an accredited Montessori training school, and the use of Montessori equipment and materials	Democratic with all inhabitants considered equal members of the community. School run by students + staff (one vote/ student; 1 vote/ staffer); all rules via school meetings/ tribunals. Officers voted in for major responsibilities	Democratic: school run by students + staff (one vote/ student; 1 vote/ staffer); all rules via school meetings. Meetings decide every school rule, who is suspended or expelled for violation, how money is spent, etc.	Teachers run school day to day, overseen by a board of teachers and parents who make decisions. There is a local governing board of overseers	Ananda, grounded in a century of Paramahansa Yogananda teachings, has 2 main campuses (California and Italy). Other Ananda-style schools are locally governed and loosely connected to the two main schools. Teachers run school day; local governance varies	Head administrator, who reports directly to the town council, works with curriculum team leaders, each of whom coordinates the efforts of teachers from five or six centers. No principal; no hierarchial relationship among teachers	Parents are autonomous. Parents who group together to share learning often join homeschool groups
MODEL	SNS New Spirituality	Montessori	Summerhill	Sudbury Valley "democratic" models	Waldorf	Ananda	Reggio Emilia	Homeschool & Unschooling

MODEL	SNS New Spirituality Learning Model	Montessori	Summerhill	Sudbury Valley "democratic" models	Waldorf	Ananda	Reggio Emilia	Homeschool & Unschooling
TEACHERS	**Teachers are seen as lead learners, teacher-guides and co-creators of the learning community circles. They discover with and guide young people rather than "teach" based on what they already know, and they provide continuous, consistent modeling of life-long learning; "leading learning" is modeled as a teaching process.**	AMI certified via yearlong training program. Not all teachers are required to be AMI certified; assistants may be trained on site w/o AMI accreditation	Summerhill seeks teachers who know how to feel, love, and allow freedom, and who embody the integration of head and heart	New teachers have a trial teaching time; then are voted in or out by students and staff	Teachers are Waldorf certified. Strong teacher-parent-child bonding is developed as teachers stays with same group of students throughout elementary school	Teachers have specialties in the classes provided	Teacher is a colearner with children – a researcher, resource, and guide. Little pre-service training required. Teacher is fairly autonomous and expected to keep developing as a skilled observer of children	No credentials required. Children are taught by parents and other family members. Experts and mentors in specific fields of study often sought. Strong parent-child bonding is often developed
KEY WORDS and/or AIMS	**Principles:** * **awareness** * **honesty** * **responsibility** * **gratitude** * **spirit/heart focused** * **Learner-Led** * **Teachers Guides/ Lead-Learners** * **Learning to live with God=Life**	* hands-on/ active * supportive learning environs * real-life materials/ activities * interaction * respect for varied learning styles	Aims: * to allow children freedom to grow emotionally * to give children power * to give children time to develop naturally * to create happier childhood by removing fear/ coercion by adults	* individuality * values * real-world problems	* intellect (as in lectures) * heart (as in artistic and feeling aspects of the subject) * hands (as in the practical application) * social renewal	universal truths of: * honesty * kindness * courage * patience * success * willpower	* environment * ability * security * self-esteem * knowledge * sevelopment (actual & potential) * responsibility	* freedom * parental choice regarding learning

Resources with more information on Alternative Learning Models:

A New Spirituality Model: www.SchooloftheNewSpirituality.com
Linda@SchooloftheNewSpirituality.com
Linda Lee Ratto, Ed.M., SNS Executive Director; www.LindaLeeRatto.com

Books on New Learning Models:
School of the New Spirituality MANUAL (The SNS STEPS downloaded comprise the 400+ page manual.)
Conversations with God, Book Two by Neale Donald Walsch
Conversations with God, Book Two Guidebook, by Anne-Marie Barbier; email directly for workshops: Blissofspirit9@cs.com
Tomorrow's god – A Guidebook by Christina Semple; email directly for workshops: SNSatlanta@SchooloftheNewSpirituality.com
Friendship with God by Neale Donald Walsch
Friendship with God – A Guidebook, by Donna Corso
Beyond Counterfeit Reforms and Total Leaders by William G. Spady, Ph.D.

Montessori Model:
www.montessori-ami.org
www.montessori.org/
www.montessori.org/Resources/LibraryMenu.htm
Tomorrow's Child Magazine
The Absorbent Mind and *The Montessori Method* by Maria Montessori

Summerhill Model:
www.summerhillschool.co.uk/
Summerhill: A Radical Approach to Child-Rearing by A.S. Neill

Sudbury Valley School "Democratic" Model:
www.sudval.org/
cedarwoodsudbury.org/reading.htm
www.cedarwoodsudbury.org/texts/okayso.htm

Waldorf Model:
www.awsna.org
www.steinerwaldorf.org.uk
www.awsna.org/education-class.html
www.skylarkbooks.co.uk/
Discussions with Teachers by Rudolph Steiner

Ananda Model:
www.ananda.org/ananda/village/
efl.org
Education for Life: Preparing Children to Meet the Challenges by J. Donald Walters

Reggio Emilia Model:
www.ericfacility.net/databases/ERIC_Digests/ed354988.html
http://ericeece.org/reggio/reschool.html
http://smartstartecec.com
Reflections on the Reggio Emilia Approach, edited by Lilian G. Katz and Bernard Cesarone
Making Learning Visible: Children as Individual and Group Learners by Project Zero and Reggio Children, USA

Homeschooling/Unschooling Model:
www.learninfreedom.org
www.awsna.org/education-class.html
www.hslda.org
NHERI.org
www.clonlara.org

More Books on Alternative Schooling:
SNS Conversations with God Guidebook, Series of 11 companion books to the *Conversations with God* books, by Neale Donald Walsch
www.SchooloftheNewSpirituality.com click media store !
www.parentbooks.ca/alternatives_education.html
www.LindaLeeRatto.com

KEY DEFINITIONS for Chapter 9:

Education (a new definition): "drawing from within," not feeding-into the student; teaching and learning specific skills, *and also something less tangible* and more profound – universal wisdom. New spirituality learning communities model 'to draw out,' facilitating realization of self-potential and inherent talents of an individual – child or adult. Education in the 21st Century is for all because all are equal souls to one another.

Curriculum: Set of courses, and their content usually offered at a school or university. As an idea, curriculum stems from the Latin word for 'race course,' referring to the course of deeds and experiences through which children grow and mature in becoming adults, the pre-learning for a career. In new spirituality learning models, a career is based on a child's innate passions and life purposes.

5 – Summary and Extension of this chapter lesson:

- It is time for adults to take responsibility for listening, hearing and supporting youth in developing together more meaningful ways to learn.

- Consider the education systems in your community. Could you help shift and enhance them, along with those children in your world?

- What did you learn about your education research? Were you surprised about what you learned? How? Why?

- Sketch a dream learning setting with the children in your life. Now may be a perfect opportunity to listen and reflect on learning *together* and see what you can *"cook-up."*

NOTE: for current information about Neale's vision, see the School of the New Spirituality program information in the Resource section.

Chapter 10

POLITICS

Chapter 10 Summary

The way governments around the world have been leading their countries is based on self interest and separation. Laws have been passed to provide for people's needs, rather than allowing people to provide for themselves. Growth is very challenging when people are constantly told what to do by their governments. Some laws are limiting because they benefit self power versus all human interest. The solution would be to just have only a few laws and allow self-governance.

We are not afraid to waste in all aspects of our lives. We pay people huge salaries in the entertainment business while children die from starvation. This chapter asks readers to consider deeply that we are all part of the human family. How can we help our fellow humans?

"Not all politics are bad, but the art of politics is a practical art. It recognizes with great candor the psychology of most people. It simply notices that most people operate out of self-interest. So politics is the way that people of power seek to convince you that their self-interest is your own."

~ Neale Donald Walsch
Conversations with God Book 2, p. 133

"In your society, if providing for the good of the many does not produce a huge profit for someone, the good of the many is more often than not ignored."

~ Neale Donald Walsch
Conversations with God Book 2, p. 138

2 – Quotes from Other Spiritual Masters

"The illusion is that your country defines who you are. The reality is that finding out who you are requires self-searching and self-knowledge."

~ Deepak Chopra, MD
Peace is the Way

3 – Principles & Objectives

Principles:

I. How can we replace self-interest by common good interest, and living "We are ONE?"

II. How can we help stop all the atrocities of the world from happening again and again?

III. The problems of human family are everyone's responsibility.

IV. One-world government could be a global solution.

V. To get to the one "global government," we must tap into the universal domain, our ONEness, our collective consciousness.

Learning Objectives:

A) You will learn how to tune in to the universal life force.

B) You will tap into the gift of being part of the human family and universal spirit.

4 – Exercises

***Conversations with God book 2,* Chapter 10- Affirmation**

"My intention is to realize that we (people of the world), have been living our lives through human laws, and we now want to live through the universal laws."

---

1. Tuning in to the universal life force:
   The destructive words we say, either out loud or in a dysfunctional internal dialogue, have a powerful, global impact. Positive, constructive thoughts and words are as powerful. We are what we believe and we may always choose differently. Our belief systems will create who we are. Our choices will be our reality.

   Write down all the positive, pro-active dream intentions you want to see happening for yourself and our world. Read theses intentions everyday, when you wake up, before your meditation practice, before eating, before bedtime. This reprograms your destructive mental recordings from the past.

   - Send the intention: I see a better world, in peace.
   - Send the intention: I see people in need have a better life.
   - Send the intention: I am a better person.
   - Send the intention: I forgive any hurting words or wrongdoing this day.
   - Send the intention: I have better self awareness and knowledge.
   - Send the intention: I am grateful for what I have in my life.
   - Send the intention: I am growing as a spiritual being.
   - Send the intention: I hold inside peace for those who are dead.
   - Send the intention: I am receiving affluence and abundance.

- Send the intention: I am peace and I desire to spread serenity.
- Send the intention: I feel safe and protected from all destructive negativity in the world.
- I have and I own non-functional thoughts, words and actions and choice constructive thoughts, words and actions to replace the old.

2. Being part of the human family:
    Treating others as you wish to be treated. Helping someone can take many forms.

    Decide to:
    - Assist an elder, a child or a person who is ill.
    - Helping someone and do not expect anything in return. Just help out of pure, genuine interest.
    - Smile to a stranger.
    - If someone acts in a rude or hurtful manner, respond with kindness and love.
    - Send those you meet the intention for each person to feel peace within.

KEY DEFINITION for Chapter 10:

Politics: the process by which groups of people make decisions on who gets what. The term is generally applied to behavior within civil governments, but politics has been observed in all human group interactions, including corporate, academic, and religious systems and communities.

Politics consists of "social relations involving authority or power" and refers to the regulation of a political unit, and to the methods and tactics used to formulate and apply policy.

5 – Summary of this chapter lesson:

- When sending caring, authentic and constructive intentions, what did you learn? How and why?

- How did it feel to experience sending kindness to someone who is rude? What kind of reaction did you receive back? Did you sense that the receiving person shifted? How? Note your observations now and as you interact again.

Chapter 11

PEACE

Chapter 11 Summary

"Need Nothing. Desire everything. Choose what shows up. Feel your feelings. Cry your cries. Laugh your laughs. Honor your truth. Yet when all emotion is done, be still and know that I am God."

~ Neale Donald Walsch
Conversations with God Book 2, p. 153

The only solution for the problems of humanity is love – there is a lack if it. A one-world government, with no separation within the humankind family, would help to feed, clothe and house everyone. This solution would not take anything from anyone. We could decide to use some of the money we spend for military needs. We would keep some of the military budget for internal purposes, such as to strengthen local police and local wellness groups.

To cancel the fear of aggression from richer nations toward nations who would want what the richer nations have, an old pattern of humanity, we could develop a new attitude toward one another, sharing enough of the world's total wealth with all the world's people and create a system for the resolution of differences that even eliminates the possibility of war.

There is already an experiment of that concept in United States of America. No one would argue that the system needs improvement, but the recipe has worked for more than 200 years. American founders used a confederation of individual states conducting localized affairs. These individual states did fight wars with each other, but ultimately the states successfully decided to unite into a cohesive group, each reporting to a central authority. They all increased profits and were able to help people because they did not have to protect individual states from each other. This is a productive, functional example of a geopolitical solution toward ONEness and world peace.

Of course, humans have differing viewpoints and may disagree. However, if there is a global shift away from attachment to outer things, because everyone would have their basic needs met – enough food, clothing and shelter – this global solution shift would be a spiritual one, combined with the geopolitical one.

For example, geopolitical solutions have been tried on a global scale with the League of Nations and most recently the United Nations. The first one failed and the second has been mired in long-time past habits of stronger nations holding onto power-over attitudes. The spiritual shift is started by a new focus on improving the quality of life for the good of all.

Shifting the world's military budget to humanitarian purposes, for example, would solve problems without shifting any of the wealth from where it is now. Some would argue that those international conglomerates and their employees, whose profits come from war, would be "losers" in this search for a solution to our world's conflict consciousness. But if one has to depend on the world living in bitter conflicts in order to survive, we could collectively choose otherwise and re-evaluate our priorities. Do we want war or peace? Do we want to live from an Outside World (physical) consciousness, or from an Inner World (spiritual) consciousness?

> "Love breeds tolerance, tolerance breed peace. Intolerance produces war and looks indifferently upon intolerable conditions."
>
> ~ Neale Donald Walsch
> *Conversation with God Book 2,* p. 142

> "It is as Winston Churchill said, 'Democracy is the worst system,' he announced, 'except all others.' "
>
> ~ Neale Donald Walsch
> *Conversation with God Book 2,* p. 146

2 – Quotes from Other Spiritual Masters

> "Peace is the way, there is no other way."
>
> ~ Gandhi
> *From "Peace is the Way"*
> By Deepak Chopra, MD

> "Right now there are 21.3 millions soldiers serving in armies around the world. Can't we recruit a peace brigade ten times larger? A hundred times large? The effort begins now, with you."
>
> ~ Deepak Chopra
> *Peace is the Way*

3 – Principles & Objectives

Principles:

I. As long as the "poor" see their unhappiness connected to the lack of material things, they will always want what the "rich" have. This is a mental, belief-based trap.

II. Wars exist because somebody wants something that someone else has and takes it.

III. A spiritual solution is the answer to avoiding war, because at the end of the day, every geopolitical strife and personal problem comes down to a spiritual issue.

IV. Inner love and peace is freedom from fear and anger.

V. Inner peace is found when we realize we need nothing.

VI. We create our outside world by our internal dialogue.

VII. There is perfection in everything, even through tragedy. We choose, we appreciate often from a comparison of what we do not want.

Learning Objectives:

A) You will learn how to deal with fear and anger from a new inner dialogue.
B) You will find solutions to help you become a peace maker.

4 – Exercises

> ### *Conversations with God book 2*, Chapter 11- Affirmation
>
> **"Even through the greatest tragedy, I can be a peace maker. I will quiet my mind and move deep within my soul."**

1. Determine whether your internal dialogue is running these kinds of thoughts:

   - I am afraid of getting old.
   - I am scared of people.
   - I can't center myself on anything.
   - I am a failure.
   - I worry all the time.
   - I can't express my feelings.
   - I fear being alone.
   - I have a bad temper.
   - Everything I try does not work for me.
   - I am scared of flying.
   - Everybody criticizes me.

If these thoughts are part of your mind's dialogue, you are exhibiting fear.
Take the time to write-out some of your everyday, destructive inner thoughts.

You can reverse the destructive process by positive, constructive affirmations:
   - The older I get, the stronger and better I feel.
   - Everywhere I go, I feel protected and secure.
   - Clarity is part of my inner vision.
   - I am a success in all aspects of my life.
   - I feel peace and harmony.
   - I can express my feelings because I know I will be heard.
   - I radiate love and love comes to me all the time.
   - I experience peace within and in my life.
   - I always find the right decision to make.
   - I feel safe and I accept my life as being perfect.
   - I feel loved and appreciated all the time.

2. Anger is a very damaging emotion, especially when you are stuck in it.
   Anger can keep you away from the Divine, from God consciousness. When you are angry, you have the motivation to hurt others, leading you to hurt yourself more than anybody else. Instead of helping you grow, hanging on to anger takes you in the opposite direction, which is going backward, not allowing your spiritual transformation. It is very important to let go this kind of emotional commotion.

   As soon as you feel the anger coming up try these 4 Steps:

   a) **Identify:** The emotion associated with the anger. It usually shows up as a sensation in the body.

   b) **Ask:** Go deeper, what kind of sensations are you feeling? Is it a pinch in the throat or at the level of the solar plexus or in the heart?

c) Take a moment to feel: What does it feel like in your body? Be fully aware of each feeling. Heart-rate, feeling hot or cold? Shivers?

d) Release: By allowing your attention to focus on the body, you release the thought process and thus begin letting go of the feeling.

Please know, anger expressed and let go quickly, is okay and is part of human nature. However, anger as a habit, expressed intensely and often can lead to hostility and continual distress. Hostility can lead to health problems like cancer, infections, or speeding the aging process.

3. To be a peace maker, think about creating peace often. *Make peace a habit.*
   - When you see a conflict happening in your own life, in your family or with your friends, do something different to create a different result.
   - Try to create an idea that would bring peace in your surroundings.
   - Try connecting with another person – laugh, have fun, choose another way other than anger.
   - Try seeing another with compassion first.
   - Show respect through trying to understand.
   - Refrain from complaints or criticism.
   - Be the peace you wish for yourself.

By fresh, new ways of connecting, you create trust, and with trust there is no need for hostility or suspicions – thus no need to use anger as a daily way to live.

KEY DEFINITIONS for Chapter 11:

Anger: feeling of displeasure; bodily reactions can be intense and if sustained, cause physical illness and damage

Hostility: a state, a condition, an attitude of *against*, rather than *flowing with* (people and life)

5 – Summary of this chapter lesson:

- We always have a choice between love and fear in any situation. We go through all kinds of anxieties and fears, especially fear of letting go of the past and fear of the future, of the unknown. We also fear taking a chance on something. We exhibit fear of intimacy by not asking people for what we desire, hoping they will guess.

- Knowing how to love ourselves leads to miracles. What did you learn in this chapter about yourself? Write a whole page on YOU.

Chapter 12

ATTITUDE

Chapter 12 Summary

An attitude held by many people is that poor people are poor because they want to be. It is their own fault that they are not successful. Is this attitude helping us all?

What would happen if we gave people the help they ask for by empowering them somehow? What you have the opportunity to do for the less fortunate is to re-mind them, that is, cause them to be a New Mind about themselves. This means our global neighbors, colleagues, and, yes, our family members can be treated and seen anew. It is a daily choice to see them as the loving spirits they are. At a metaphysical level, no one is disadvantaged, given what the soul wants to accomplish – co-creation of the grandest version of the greatest vision of self. We create every day and see the opposite of what we desire every day. This is the way life works.

To create anew, and know Who You Are in your experience consider:

1. Relativity
2. Forgetfulness
3. Consciousness

Being in service to others is a beautiful way of life rather than something imposed by others such as your family, your work group, or even a government.

"It is the act of God being God. It is Me being Me – through you ! This is the point of all life. Through you, I experience being Who and What I Am. Without you, I could know it, but not experience it."

~ Neale Donald Walsch
Conversations with God, p. 159

"Remember that the greatest help you can give a person is to wake them up, to remind them of Who They Really Are. There are many ways to do this. Sometimes with a little bit of help; a push, a shove, a nudge…"

~ Neale Donald Walsch
Conversations with God, p. 159

---

2 – Quotes from Other Spiritual Masters

"We are commanded not to kill, but over sixteen thousand people are murdered each year in the United States, and, in the name of God or country, tens of thousands are killed in armed conflicts. We are commanded not to steal, but over ten million thefts occur annually. We have a prohibition against adultery, yet studies suggest that at least half of married people engage in extramarital affairs. Treated as children, people respond as children. It is time to replace commandment with commitment."

~ David Simon
The Ten Commitments

3 – Principles & Objectives

Principles:

I.   Attitude is a reflection of our inner beliefs.

II. Love and Compassion first, especially when in doubt.

III. The challenge facing humankind is to provide each and everyone with basic survival needs with dignity; then all may choose what more they want from there.

IV. We have Enough. Shifts in consciousness happen in our hearts, rather than looking outwardly for *other than self* means (such as governmental or political means).

Learning Objectives:

A) You will discover how to transform good intentions into good choices.
B) You will learn how to share a change in consciousness.

4 – Exercises

Conversations with God book 2, Chapter 12- Affirmation

"My intention is to experience goodness in my heart, fairness in my mind, love in my soul."

In order to transform good intentions into good choices, we need to discover, clarify and release negative, destructive behaviors and replace them with positive, wellness ones.

1. Take your journal and write down all the habits that are obstacles to your physical and emotional health and well-being. Write free-flow or in lists, but put into words what you wish to see more change in your life. Now ask: what you really need and want to change now? Write your desires down in clear, short, concise words.

VISUALIZE YOU by Being in Your Own "Audience"
Knowing what your changeable habits are, bring your full attention to those moments of mindless habit. For example, if you smoke, before lighting a cigarette, be fully aware of what you are doing: Look at the color of the cigarette pack, observe yourself pulling the cigarette out from the cigarette pack, look at the paper, the tobacco colors, smell the cigarette, feel the cigarette in your fingers. When you light it, see the flame before it reaches the cigarette, observe the flame when it unites with the cigarette, smell the smoke. Feel the heat enter your lips… Just be the silent witness. Observe without judging. This will allow you to be in the moment, not in the past or the future, in the moment of choicemaking and change.

2. Now send the intention to visualize the changes you want to see in your life, again for example a smoker might ask:

   - Will I get healthier?
   - How will it feel to be *more well?*
   - Will I cough less?
   - Will I taste food differently?
   - Will my clothes smell unlike cigarettes?
   - Will my skin look brighter?
   - Will my energy pick up?
   - Will my house smell differently?
   - Will I save money? How much?
   - What might I save as a result of not purchasing my "habit tools"?

3. Decide on a date you will change your destructive behavior. Prepare your days ahead of time by writing a daily schedule to help you in that change. Clear your house of what is unwanted and ask for support from family and friends. To clear an old habit, replace it with an activity that will be fulfilling. For example, decide to take yoga classes, start going for walks, drink lots of water, eat healthy food, get a massage, or go to bed early for deeper rest. It is very helpful to stay away from people who will not support your willingness to change your behavior. If you stop smoking, stay away from people who still do. Try making a new friend.

   Day by day, choice by choice you feel better about yourself. The better you feel about yourself, the more you will be able to have more compassion and understanding for others. This is a fundamental pathway to world peace, from the inside – out.

4. Next steps – Give away that which you seek

   - Engage yourself with an association of your choice that will bring you joy because you will be able to help other people who truly are seeking love and care.

- Look in your local newspapers or telephone book and notice organizations that address missions, topics or causes you love.
- Go on-line and see what associations might be of deep interest. Make your choice and go for one new personal involvement.
- Discover the beauty of sharing a change in consciousness. Go to www.SchooloftheNewSpirituality.com and learn how to open a simple book or movie group to start your journey.

KEY DEFINITION for Chapter 12:

Attitude: an individual's like or dislike; an underlying belief- positive, negative or neutral toward a person, behavior or event. Change in attitude starts with walking *as if* a belief has changed.

5 – Summary and Extension of this chapter lesson:

- Attitudes are composed from various forms of judgments.
- Attitudes develop according to an easy to remember **ABC** model:
    1. **A**ffect

    Affective response is a physiological response that expresses an individual's preference for a person or event.

    2. **B**ehavioral change

    Behavioral intention shows, in a verbal or body language way, indications of the deeper intentions of an individual.

    3. **C**ognition, mental understanding

    Cognitive response is a mental judgment to form an attitude. Most attitudes are a result of observational learning from those around us.

- When writing down all the habits that are obstacles to your physical and emotional health and wellbeing, what did you learn about the inner workings of YOU?
- Make a note, short and sweet, concisely stating your learning. Post it somewhere in your home to allow these personal revelations to come into form in new ways, on a daily basis, as you pass and read this note containing your new information – your new self-awarenesses.

Chapter 13

LOVE

Chapter 13 Summary

Express love in all you do. Be a model of the Highest Truth within you, that we are the essence and spirit of Love, Joy and Wisdom in human form.

> "Be a light unto the world, and hurt it not. Seek to build, not to destroy."
> ~ Neale Donald Walsch
> *Conversations with God, p. 175*

> "Be a gift to everyone who enters your life, and to everyone whose life you enter. Be careful not to enter another's life if you cannot be a gift."
> ~ Neale Donald Walsch
> *Conversations with God, p. 176*

2 – Quotes from Other Spiritual Masters

> "The secret to being attractive, if one consults the past record of human experience, it is remarkably simple. It is summarized in an aphorism from the Latin poet Ovid, who said, "To love, be lovable." A lovable person is someone who is natural, easy with himself or herself, radiating the simple, unaffected humanity that makes anyone truly attractive."
> ~ Deepak Chopra, MD
> *The Path to Love*

3 – Principles & Objectives

Principle:

Through love, we can accomplish everything.

Learning Objective:

You will learn how to love yourself and how to love others.

4 – Exercises

Conversations with God book 2, Chapter 13- Affirmation
"I am loving, loved and lovable."

1. Make a list of things you love; for example things like:
   - Beauty of nature
   - Joy of being healthy
   - Support of friends and family
   - Loving animals
   - Loving how your mind works
   - Thrilling in the country you live
   - Relishing the universe and how it works.

2. Now remember your list items:
   - Bless your current life with love.
   - Be aware – stop and drink in your loves
   - Experience a little more time to love a little more each time that you are in a situation described in your list above.
   - BE in love with your life.

KEY DEFINITION for Chapter 13:

Love: represents a range of human emotions and experiences related to the senses of affection and also sexual attraction; can refer to a variety of different feelings, states, and attitudes, ranging from generic pleasure to intense interpersonal attraction.

As an abstract concept, love usually refers to a strong, ineffable feeling towards another person or activity. Even this limited conception of love, however, encompasses a wealth of different feelings, from the passionate desire and intimacy of romantic love to the nonsexual forms of creativity. Love in its various forms acts is a major facilitator of interpersonal relationships. It is one of the most common themes in the creative arts, for passion and love shine through these deeply personal endeavors. Writing, painting, drawing, music, dance, are a few examples.

5 – Summary and Extension of this chapter lesson:

A) Before we can show love and compassion for anyone, we need to love the self. Too often, we don't realize how unloving we are *toward ourselves*. From criticism to saying unconstructive things like "I'm stupid," we can actually decide to believe that we are not lovable. We get involved in toxic relationships. We hurt our bodies with addictions such as food, cigarettes, alcohol, drugs. *We can choose other than what we have been choosing.*

- Write down how this paragraph feels to you after you have read it over a few times.

B) Look back at the time period since you started this chapter's activities. Answer:

- How am I doing?
- Are my non-functional habits shifting a little? A lot?
- How am I feeling about doing something new?
  - Uneasy?
  - Nervous?
  - Moving forward *as if* I am changed?

C) Please take the time to write and identify why you feel good or not-so-good about changing your habit. Keep self-reflecting, through writing, as you work and live toward growth and change for your highest good.

Chapter 14

HELP + EMPOWERMENT

Chapter 14 Summary

A life paradox: Help given to someone with what *you think is needed* will produce dependency. Yet can we ignore someone in need? Helping is really a receiving conversation between a listener who assists by doing what another is ready to accept.

> "Never offer the kind of help that disempowers. Never insist on offering the help you think is needed. Let the person or people in need know all that you have to give – then listen to what they want. See what they are ready to receive."
>
> ~ Neale Donald Walsch
> *Conversations with God Book 2, p. 178*

2 – Principles & Objectives

Principles:
(Core new ideas for the world, according to Neale Donald Walsch)

I.   Helping others fulfill their wishes is a sure way that you will be able to accomplish your own dreams. This is the Law of Attraction.

II. We are here to give happiness to all human beings that we encounter, including self.

Learning Objective:

You will learn how to help by empowering those around you. These learnings can transform humanity.

3 – Exercises

> *Conversations with God book 2*, Chapter 14- Affirmation
>
> **"I will help through empowerment and listening carefully. I will not ignore anyone who is seeking help. "**

---

1. Make a commitment to listen. You will hear how you can help people. Especially hear your family members, your friends, your co-workers, and your neighbors.

2. Regardless of what kind of help people need, do not make any judgment on the situation; listen and decide to assist *on their terms.*

3. See what kind of solutions you can offer and allow the person to decide what s/he is ready for. You cannot force help on anyone and it is not your role to rescue anyone, either. Each one of us acts from his/her own level of awareness. Every human being must be accepted with compassion *where they are.*

KEY DEFINITION for Chapter 14

Empowerment: increasing the spiritual, emotional, physical, political, social, or economic strength of individuals and communities; often involves the empowered developing confidence capacities as individuals and collectives.

5 – Summary of this chapter lesson:

If, indeed, it is a natural way of life to evolve toward growth and development, then we must continually ask ourselves: is what we are doing bringing happiness to ourselves and the people around us?

- Help will be most useful when you provide some choices of things you can do for someone and let them ask you what they want and are willing to receive.
- Make a List of those you wish to especially listen to and eventually help:

Name	Need	Your Approach to Listening
1. your loved one or friend		I will meet and ask
2.		
3.		
4.		
5.		

- What can you or did you learn about allowing another person to choose the help they desire? How did it make you feel? Why?

- Allowing others to choose their guidance and assistance from you:

  - Is this a new attitude or way of living for you?
  - Why?
  - Where or from whom did you get the old attitude?
  - What truly works for you in your life now here – the old or a new attitude with a fresh underlying belief?

Chapter 15

I LOVE YOU

Chapter 15 Summary

LOVE. THAT'S ALL THERE IS.

> "I love you, you know that?
> I know you do. And I love you."
>
> ~Neale Donald Walsch
> *Conversations with God Book 2, p. 180*

"Love, Love, Love. Love, Love, Love. Love is all you need." ~ The Beatles, 1960's

2 – Quotes from Other Spiritual Masters

> "Life is love and love is life. What keeps the body together but love? What is desire but love of the self? And what is knowledge but love of truth?
>
> Deepak Chopra, MD
> *The Path to Love*

3 – Principles and Objectives

Principle:

Speaking in a humble, soft, gentle, open, candid, respectful way, is a gift of love.

Learning Objective:

You will learn how to speak in a peaceful, careful way.

4 – Exercises:

> ### *Conversations with God book 2*, Chapter 15- Affirmation
>
> **"I want to express love in all I do and not surrender to fear, anger nor violence."**

---

1. Reviewing Nonviolent Communication helps:
   - Individuals break patterns of thinking that lead to arguments, anger, and depression.
   - Families and couples communicate with mutual respect and understanding.
   - School systems create healthy respect for diversity and differences.
   - Businesses increase goodwill and cooperation with co-workers and customers.
   - Health-care professionals develop systems that support compassion.
   - Social service agencies find ways to meet needs constructively.
   - Police, military and prison personnel prevent and peacefully resolve conflicts.

2. To learn how to speak in a peaceful way, go to the book store and buy this fundamental resource *Nonviolent Communication (NVC)* by Marshall B. Rosenberg, PhD in books or audio. See the End Notes for more.

3. Use Dr. Rosenburg's "NVC" awarenesses to create a new way to speak and embody peace. Make another list. This one articulates how violence has been a part of your past, as it has been for most cultures on the earth stage for many millennia:

Your Age	Violent Event	Another Way to Have Responded in Peace

just name a few, that is all

KEY DEFINITIONS for Chapter 15

Nonviolent Communication, Peaceful Communication: lost language of humankind, the language of people who care about one another and long to live in harmony. NVC information shifts families, communities, world systems by simply one person using the techniques. Imagine what can be accomplished by creating Peace at Home in every household, every town !

Peace Leaders:
Expertise for over thirty five years, Dr. Marshall Rosenberg travels the world promoting peaceful communications. James Twyman, another peace author and also an accomplished musician, has achieved the New York Times best seller status affecting the world through his most recent book *The Moses Code,* spring 2008. Of course,

Mahatma Gandhi and Mother Theresa are Master Peace Leaders of our time for over a century !

5 – Summary of this chapter lesson:

In peaceful communication:
- We honestly express how we are *without judgment, blaming or criticizing.*
- We empathically receive *how others are* without hearing blame or criticism.

The four steps in Nonviolent Communication are:

1. Observing, with no judgment to what is
2. Feeling, name those feelings
3. Expressing needs/desires
4. Expressing requests to meet needs

Extend your peaceful learning by daily prayer or meditation and deep quiet time and also by *speaking peacefully on purpose* whenever possible.

Chapter 16

VISIBILITY

Chapter 16 Summary

We are damaging the environment. We are out of balance pertaining to money, food, shelter, and environment. As a result, fairness, equity and honesty are often not possible. If all transactions were made visible, discrimination and imbalance would not be possible. The current systems in place across the world are based on *taking advantage* of our environment, of others, of situations *to win*. There can be other ways to live together.

A visibility system would allow human beings to communicate more clearly and benefit in terms of "win-win or for the highest good of all" situations. One kind of visibility system would allow all of our thoughts, reactions, anxieties, or deepest pains to be shared and thus revealed, and then released for the highest good of all. Many of us walk in fear every day – fear of loss, fear of not enough, fear of _____ you fill-in the blank.

"Think of it. If you knew exactly how much money each of you holds and the real earnings of all of your industries and corporations and each of their executives – as well as how each person and corporation is using the money it has – don't you think that would change things?"

~ Neale Donald Walsch
Conversations with God Book 2, p. 185

"Yet the good news is that there is no reason for fear, no cause to be scared. No one is going to judge you, no one is going to make you "wrong", no one is going to throw you into the everlasting fires of hell."

~ Neale Donald Walsch
Conversations with God Book 2, p. 191

---

2 – Quotes from Other Spiritual Masters

> "A man who is swayed by passions may have good enough intentions, may be truthful in word, but he will never find the Truth. A successful search for Truth means complete deliverance from the dual throng such as of love and hate, happiness and misery."
>
> ~ Gandhi
> *An Autobiography, p. 345*

3 – Principles & Objectives

Principles:

I. Inequality could be eliminated through new money cultures and creating an international monetary system that is visible, traceable, accountable.

> More Info: One new money system could be a Worldwide Compensation System with credit given to people for services and products produced, and debit for services and products utilized. Such a system would provide complete know-ability (visibility).

II. Let us have no income tax. A voluntary deduction of ten percent of all earnings each year could be deducted from incomes to support all government programs and services.

III. If you can be physically naked with your loved one, why not be emotionally naked, too?

Learning Objective:

You will learn how to start implementing this new visibility, new truth and transparency thought systems right away.

4 – Exercises

Conversations with God book 2, **Chapter 16- Affirmation**

"I will surrender to a complete change in my thinking pattern about visibility. I will begin to build this New Society today, in my family, with my friends and at the workplace."

---

1. Take your journal and start answering these questions:

- What are you saying to someone that is not true?
- What are you keeping from others that you don't want them to know?
- Do you think you could live a life with no secrets? If not, why not?

2. Once you have answered those questions, go to a mirror and pretend you have the person or the groups of people (you wrote in your chart above) in front of you. Now speak. Tell them the truth. Know that you are and do feel safe, protected, and fully secure. Speak to the mirror all of your truths, all of your "secrets."

3. Now go directly to one or more of these people or groups you have enumerated and start telling them your truth face to face. Know that you are and do feel fully and deeply safe, protected and secure, because you always are these.

KEY DEFINITION for Chapter 16:

Happiness: emotion in which one experiences feelings ranging from contentment and satisfaction to bliss and intense joy.

Secure: condition of feeling protected against danger or loss; this feeling can eliminate fear. In the general sense, security is a concept similar to safety. In new spirituality terms, we are all always secure and safe because life is without end.

5 – Summary and Extension of this chapter lesson:

- God does not judge, so neither do you have to judge self or others.

- Ask:

    o Now that I have started to apply a truth-based, no secrets, visibility way of living system in my life, what has happened? Detail this answer.
    o Do I think that visibility brings equity and fair play into my home, with friends or in my workplace? How?
    o What did I learn by sharing my truth with at least myself?
    o What did I learn by sharing my truth with at least one other person?

- Please take time every day or two for self-reflection, so you may pave the way to a daily practice and higher personal awareness of truth and visibility. This is a pathway to newfound freedom !

Chapter 17

"WAR, NO MORE !"

Chapter 17 Summary

Disagreement between nations is a healthy sign of individuality. However, violent resolution of disagreements is an unevolved, immature way of living.

A solution to avoid war could be a One World Government with a World Court to settle disputes and a World Peacekeeping Force to guarantee that no nation can ever aggress another.

Each nation in the world would be part of the total group of 160 nations. If one nation is threatened, all other nations would collaborate for a solution and collectively say NO to war of any type, physical, emotional, or economical. The independence of individual nations would actually increase. All nations would be ethically required to share resources more equitably.

A short-term solution to world imbalance is a new, worldwide government. Some of our leaders have been courageous enough to propose the beginnings of a global government: George Bush, Mikhail Gorbachev, and Jimmy Carter, to name three. However there is far more on which to agree. People and their cultures have been light-years behind these leader's wholistic visions and saw only loss from these global concepts.

"There is no reason in the world why violent resolution cannot be avoided, given the willingness of nations to avoid it."

~ Neale Donald Walsch
Conversations with God Book 2, p. 195

"Thus it will always be until a long-term solution, which is not a political one, is put into place. That long-term solution – and the only real one – is a New Awareness and a New Consciousness. An awareness of Oneness and a consciousness of Love."

~ Neale Donald Walsch
Conversations with God Book 2, p. 200

2 – Background Information & Quotes from Other Spiritual Masters

"When a person is established in nonviolence, those in his vicinity cease to feel hostility."

~ Patanjali, ancient Indian sage
From *"Peace is the Way"*
by Deepak Chopra, MD

3 – Principles & Objectives

Principles:

I. To provide equal opportunity to each person and nation, for the highest good of humanity, would mean to detach from holding tightly to control.

II. Outsourcing, or looking outwardly for desires and dreams, could be eliminated if peace and harmony began and was sustained from the inside, out.

III. Is a higher definition of "living a better life" an accumulation of all the world's material things? Consider that this definition promotes a deeper trap into war, conflict and 'better-than.'

IV. Is a higher definition of "living a better life" to bring peace and love power into the world to replace conflict, hatred and despair? This is a collective way to higher states of being.

Learning Objectives:

You will learn how to be a peacemaker in all aspects of your life.

4 – Exercises

Conversations with God book 2, Chapter 17- Affirmation

"I AM a peacemaker."

Protests against wars have not been working. The simple fact that someone stands in front of a government building to protest against war or against a crazy despot, creates more violence. Dreams of conflict and war in the world are counterproductive at best. In our hearts, we condemn acts of violence and we don't understand how people are so willing to go to war. However, we have a tendency to act, from past learned behaviors, in a violent manner in all aspects of our lives. As long as violence is a choice of our lives, we will attract that violence.

What are you doing that brings violence into your life? Are you willing to do something to shift your behavior? Consider what Mother Theresa said countless times, "I will not walk in a parade against war, but if you have *a parade for peace,* I'll be there."

1. In your journal write every violent act that you have done in your life. Keep writing in quick phrases what comes to mind.

   Here are some questions to help:

   - Have you ever yelled at another car on the highway because it was going too slow?
   - Have you yelled or spanked your children?
   - Have you ever pushed someone in a crowd?
   - Do you hold grudges and do not forgive?
   - Have you ever had violent thoughts against someone you did not like?
   - Have you ever told yourself that you were stupid, or some other unloving words?
   - If you have a business, have you ever forced employees to work long hours to finish a project?

We can also be violent to and with our bodies.
   - Have you ever mistreated your body by smoking, drinking alcohol, eating too much food? When our internal dialogue is focused on violence, violence will be ready to explode around us. We attract what we are.

2. After finishing your list, take a moment to think and feel about what you could do to change the way you feel about these listed circumstances. For instance, instead of yelling at a driver because she was going below the speed limit, take a moment to notice the stress you are causing yourself and shift your thinking to what the driver might be feeling. You may sense that the person is lost and confused. If you transform your thinking pattern into patience and compassion toward that driver, you will be rewarded by a good feeling. This is being empathetic.

KEY DEFINITION for Chapter 17:

Violence: forceful human destruction of property or injury to persons, often intentional though not always, and forceful verbal and emotional abuse that cause harm to self or others. Johan Galtung defines violence as "avoidable insult to basic human needs": survival, well being, identity, and freedom.

5 – Summary of this chapter lesson:

- Some global imbalances and consequences of "living a better life" based on the accumulation of things are:

   1 – High percentage of the world population is struggling for physical survival.
   2 – A smaller amount of people can provide for the basics of survival by working hard, yet concerned about getting more for a better tomorrow.
   3 – A small number of people have everything they desire, yet their minds are preoccupied with getting even more and more
   4 – Another small group of people is detached from the need to acquire material things. This group is concerned with other than material, earthly things and spiritual experiences.

- Now that you have pondered and realized that the long-term solution against war is an Awareness of Oneness and a consciousness of Love, what have you noticed about the way violence may show up in your life? Had you ever thought about your own violence? How did it make you feel? Write, draw and otherwise document your violent experiences and those you have turned-into peacefulness.

Chapter 18

EQUAL OPPORTUNITY

Chapter 18 Summary

The mission of a new world government would be to provide equal opportunity to human beings, as Neale writes and envisions in this chapter. All these concepts are not to be taken as gospel or doctrine. These ideas are exposed to stimulate thinking. You always create your own reality.

Two changes to occur to accomplish this new world government mission are:
- A shift in the political paradigm
- A shift in the spiritual paradigm

A world federation would
1. End wars between nations
2. End poverty
3. End destruction of the Earth
4. End struggle "for more"
5. Provide equal opportunity to the highest expression of Self
6. Create Abundance for All and end limitations in all aspects of life

Nothing would stop people from collecting benefits and lollygagging around. We would not resent or judge those who would not work if we were enlightened because we would understand that those who are not contributing would miss out on the most wonderful journey of discovering *Who They Really Are.*

Workplace could be called "Joy Place." We would still be going through emotions such as envy and jealousy. Envy is a motivator and jealousy is a fear-driven emotion.

The never-ending greatness of human spirit would guarantee that we'll have enough contributors to "carry" to non-contributors.

Financial earnings would be limited and a 10% of income would be given voluntary to the world government. These limits would not be required. The consciousness shift on the planet for its highest purpose would be the motivation to participate.

"For all the world's magnificence, you have not found a way to be magnificent enough to stop people from starving to death, much less stop killing each other. You actually let children starve to death right in front of you. You actually kill people because they disagree with you. You are primitive."

~ Neale Donald Walsch
Conversations with God Book 2, p. 204-205

"And here is the one thing you still apparently do not grasp: you are creating it all – all of your life – right here, right now. You... YOU... are creating it. Not Me... YOU."

~ Neale Donald Walsch
Conversations with God Book 2, p. 215

2 – Principles & Objectives

Principles:
(Core new ideas for the world, according to Neale Donald Walsch)

I. The world government would guarantee
   1. Basic needs provided for everyone
   2. An opportunity to accomplish more

II. The world government could be set up as follows:

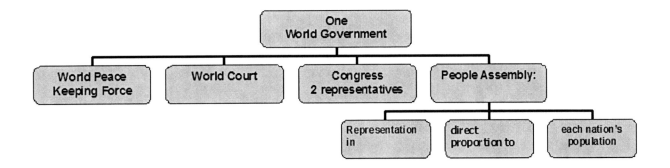

The new world order would not require anything. It would provide:
- Proper education for enjoyable careers
- Healthcare for everyone
- Housing, food and clothing for everyone
- Basic dignities of life to humanity

Learning Objectives:

A) You will learn more about the way our system is set up right now.
B) You will learn how to share your ideas of a better world.

3 – Exercises

> ***Conversations with God book 2**, Chapter 18- Affirmation*
>
> **"I will share my desire to see a better world with as many people as possible."**

1. Go on-line or otherwise research for political, economical, financial, social information about the system in which you live and work, as it is right now. This exercise is for a higher understanding of what is going on. Change happens when you name what is to be changed.

2. Share your understanding of a better life with someone else who is as interested as you are about a changing, growing world.

3. Create or attend some gatherings through different associations to discuss your ideas. You could call these gatherings "Café-Philo" (philosophy-café) or some other name if you wish. Share your developing ideas and invite others to dialogue those ideas.

4. Dare to contact some political figures and meet with them. Discuss your growing experience of a better world. Invite them to think about your ideas and give you feedback.

KEY DEFINITION for Chapter 18:

"Café-Philo": original practice of philosophy, born in Paris in December 1992 at Cafe des Phares, Place de la Bastille, with the philosopher Marc Sautet, who led a public discussion every Sunday morning at 11am. "Café-Philo" acquired a great popularity, thanks to Marc Sautet's charisma and the fact that the phenomenon attracted many others, including the media.

The spirit that prevails in a "café-philo" is that of tolerance, openness and pluralism, which makes it a unique practice to democratic societies. Founder, Marc Sautet, wanted his open philosophy to take its place among the debates of contemporary society, as an instrument of critical thought and freedom, to promote alertness and lucidity among responsible citizens.

5 – Summary of this chapter lesson:

- You don't need to earn anything, not even your way into God's graces. Everything is already available on earth to give and receive.

- You have shared your ideas with others, you dared to contact political figures: how does it make you feel? Do you feel the true power within, versus waiting for some external power? What else do you feel?

Extension of this Chapter

Consider, as Neale posits at the end of this chapter, to see the potential of our world economy and its staggering luxuries as Abundance ! See this life as the sea of possibilities that it is. Choose a way of balancing the Abundance for all, attracting even more Abundance, *by consciously, every day evolving your own Abundance through giving and exchanging with those around you.*

Chapter 19

INCREASING SPIRITUAL AWARENESS

Chapter 19 Summary

Our economic, political, social, and religious systems are primitive. However, we think they are not and we have a hard time believing that we can improve.

What we have created so far on our planet is elementary, child-like and primitive. Some examples from the San Francisco Chronicle, on Saturday, April 9 1994:
1. Nations refuse to grant basic rights to workers.
2. The rich get richer and the poor get poorer in the face of a depression in Germany.
3. The government has to force property owners to obey fair housing laws in the United States.
4. A powerful leader tells political opponents, "I'll have you rot in jail ! I'll tear your beard out hair by hair !" while punching them in the face on the floor of the national legislature in Russia.
5. Civilians suffer most in Angolan civil war: "In rebel areas, top guns live in luxury while many thousands starve."

Our civilization, over and over again, has asked, "Where did we go wrong?" "How can we do better?" The Universe has shown us its observations over and over again. We keep ignoring them. The teacher shows up when the student is ready. It is up to us to make the changes, now and here.

We have been visited by extraterrestrial beings to assist us in technology, for instance. There has been a huge "comprehension explosion" within the past 100 years alone.

"I am saying that the struggle between the "haves" and the "have-nots" has been going on forever and is epidemic on your planet. It will ever be thus so long as economic interests, rather than humanitarian interests, run the world – so long as man's body, and not man's soul, is man's highest concern."

~ Neale Donald Walsch
Conversations with God Book 2, p. 227

"What you think is what you get. What you fear is what you will draw to you. What you resist, persists. What you look at disappears – giving you a chance to recreate it all over again, if you wish, or banish it forever from your experience. What you choose, you experience."

~ Neale Donald Walsch
Conversations with God Book 2, p. 240

2 – Quotes from Other Spiritual Masters

"Your vision will become clear only when you can look into your own heart. Who looks outside dreams, who looks inside awakens."

~ Carl Jung

3 – Principles & Objectives

Principles:

I. Evolved beings know that if you are violent, people get hurt. If you keep violence going, people get angry. If you keep getting people angry, they will start hurting you back. Therefore, if you hurt someone else, sooner or later, you'll get hurt.

II. There is a consciousness shift happening right now among writers, artists, teachers, shamans, gurus, politicians, doctors, lawyers, moms and dads, grandmothers and great-grandfathers.

III. It won't take a calamity or a disaster of huge proportions to cause a massive consciousness shift, but it could. We can decide consciously to choose well.

IV Increasing the spiritual awareness of the entire planet is a slow process. It takes generations, or it can take moments.

V. What you think is what you get.

THOUGHT ⟶ WORD ⟶ ACTION IN THE WORLD

Learning Objectives:

You will learn how to increase spiritual awareness.

4 – Exercises

***Conversations with God book 2*, Chapter 19- Affirmation**
"I commit to take the opportunity to live out my own destiny. My consciousness will create the results."

In November of 2000, Deepak Chopra led a seminar in India called "How to Know God." For that occasion, he created a very helpful acronym: **L E A D E R S**. This acronym provides some additional tools to help us increase our spiritual awareness.

Look
Empowerment
Awareness
Doing
Entering the realm of creativity
Responsibility
Synchronicity (beyond coincidence)

Choose a partner to share spiritual progress with each other while practicing these exercises.

A. LOOK:

I AM A SILENT OBSERVER OF MY OWN SELF,
of my reactions, behaviors, internal reactions to situations, circumstances, people and events.

Krishnamurti (A PHILOSOPHER) once said that the highest form of human intelligence is the ability to observe without evaluation, judgment, labels, defining or analyzing.
If you do that you will be FREE.

- Observe your reactions silently without labeling them. At a subconscious level, you will automatically know when you are in an anger, fear or anxiety mode. Just knowing that is to be FREE of that. You will feel the discomfort in the body.
- Witness that discomfort by feeling the body.

B. EMPOWERMENT:

I HAVE SELF POWER

There are 2 kinds of power:
- Self power
- Ego power where your power comes from outside (political office, money, connections, somebody you know.) It is fleeting, non-lasting.

Abraham Maslow studied the traits of self-actualized, self-confident people.
- Internal dialogue comes from self power versus ego power.
- Independence is free of the opinions of others. You can't make them feel good if you flatter them, nor put them down.
- Beneath no one; Feel they are neither superior nor inferior to anyone.
- Immune to criticism
- Fearless facing challenges; they welcome challenges as an opportunity for creativity.
- Have self power; it is obvious within 30 seconds of meeting them, not because they say something, not because they do something, but because of who they are.

Emerson, the great transcendentalist, once said:
"Who you are shouts so loudly to my ears, I cannot hear what you are saying."
- It is reflected in the eyes of the person.
- It is reflected in their body language.
- And our eyes and our body language are a direct result of our internal dialogue.

Exercises:
A. SEE and Be Technique:
Close your eyes.
Repeat 3 phrases in your mind:
- I am immune to criticism
- I am beneath no one
- I am fearless
Repeat 6 times and wait 4 minutes.
Open your eyes.

B. MIRROR REMINDER
Use the following technique for the next 6 weeks, because, from psychological study, we know if you do something for 6 weeks consistently, it becomes a habit:
Every time you go by a mirror, look at your own eyes and mentally repeat
"I am immune to criticism, I am beneath no one, I am fearless."
Your eyes and body language will reflect this internal dialogue and people will respond to it perhaps not consciously, but subconsciously, because they will sense that your internal dialogue is not coming from the ego but from the level of spirit, of personally-held belief.

C. AWARENESS:

I AM SELF AWARE

C. Relax in Silence (twice a day for 20 minutes.) Before Silence, ask the questions:
- Who am I?
- What do I want?
- What is my life purpose?

You don't need to know the answers to those questions or even look for the answers. The virtual domain will make you act in circumstances, as if you know the answers and spontaneous right actions will occur.

D. DOING:

I AM ACTION-ORIENTED

- Being action oriented is to be a role model for your actions.
- I am action oriented in what? In the fulfillment of desires.
- Doing means having clarity.

D. Write down your desires:
- On the material level, it applies to things you want in life.
- On the level of sensory gratification in any form such as the 5 senses: sound, touch (sensuality, sexuality), sight, taste, smell.
- On the emotional level such as relationships
- On the spiritual level: wanting to go the whole way to experience higher states of consciousness. Do I have a Soul? What happens when I die?

E. Define your desires and create **S M A R T:**

Stretch is greater than your reach. If you think 100 miles, plan 1000. If you think 1000 miles, plan 10 000.
Measurable goals
Agreement with a partner that you have worthy goals
Record your progress along the way and share with partner
Time limit to be set, but be detached from the outcome, and know that you can always change the time limit.

Intention is supported by infinite organizing power.

E. ENTERING THE REALM OF CREATIVITY:

I AM A CO-CREATOR OF MY LIFE

F. In every moment of my life, the world that I encounter is a reflection of myself.
So, if I don't like the world that I encounter, the solution is not out there, it's in here and what's the solution? Any time there is something I don't like about my life, ask the question: "What can I do to co-create something magnificent out of this?" Write these ideas in your journal

The 9 steps of the creative response:
Conscious steps:
- Intended outcome
- Information gathering
- Information analysis
- Information processing (in rest and silence)

Spontaneous steps:
- Insight
- Inspiration
- Implementation
- Integration
- "I" – a New Me

F. RESPONSIBILITY:

I AM RESPONSIBLE

G. Address these talents for yourself and with your partner:
- Ability to respond.
- Respond creatively to everyday situations.
- Taking initiative; willing to take a risk.
- Walking your talk.
- Ask for feedback from your partner: ask your partner: "please remind me." It's OK not to walk your talk but you keep asking for feedbacks.
- Declare your values (Chopra Center values: Healing, Transformation, Service, Love)
- Integrity: nothing to hide

G. SYNCHRONICITY: (beyond coincidence)

I AM ALERT TO SYNCHRONICITY

H. It means that when a coincidence occurs, I ask myself:
- "What is the life trying to tell me?" I don't need to know the answer right away.
- Never ignore a coincidence, understand that a coincidence is a clue from life to move us to a higher level.

5 – Summary and Extension of this chapter lesson:

- We have the freedom to co-create our experiences with God at all times.

- While sharing and comparing the progress of your experiences with a partner of your choice, what surfaced? List profound feelings, emotions and especially note surprises.

- What did you learn about yourself? How? Why?

- Answer: can you remain in the awareness of your choices more often, as you notice the universe bringing you synchronicities every day?

Chapter 20

RELIGION AND SPIRITUALITY

Chapter 20 Summary

We have been told by the people holding the power, power which is ours unconsciously or consciously given away, that we need to doubt ourselves. This belief in doubt pervades our cultures

World problems and conflicts as individuals would be solved if we could:
1. Abandon the concept of Separation
2. Adopt the concept of Visibility and Oneness

The concept of abandoning Separation and adopting the concept of Visibility will take courage and determination and focused intention.

When we are totally enlightened, some of us will decide to return to the physical domain, the field of molecules, to assist others in seeing the light of truth.

Consider that organized Religion has:
- Created agnostics
- Filled many hearts with fear of God
- Ordered people to bow down before God instead of rising up
- Burdened believers with worries
- Told people to be ashamed of their bodies
- Taught that one "needed" an intermediary (priest, minister, official of the church) to reach God instead of living life by directly connecting to the Divine
- Commanded humans to practice fear-based devotion to God, instead of just adoring God because it was impossible not to
- Separated wo/men from God and placed God unreachable and above them
- Insisted that women are less than men

"God's greatest gift is the sharing of God's power."

~ Neale Donald Walsch
Conversations with God Book 2, p. 249

"In My purest form I am the Absolute. I am absolutely Everything, and therefore, I need, want, and demand absolutely nothing. From this absolutely pure form, I am as you make Me."

~ Neale Donald Walsch
Conversations with God Book 2, p. 249

2 – Quotes from Other Spiritual Masters

"My instinct is to follow the model of Satsang, which is a simple gathering for the purpose of speaking about truth. In Church, people are included if they conform to a body of rules and beliefs. In Satsang, anyone can attend who has a love of spirit; there are no obligations because there is no official organization with an agenda. A Satsang can even be silent, or it can combine a period for meditation and a period for talking."

~ Deepak Chopra
The Third Jesus

3 – Principles & Objectives

Principles:

I. Fear will be the greatest enemy in the process of abandoning Separation until we realize that what we do to others is what we do to ourselves. There is no Separation !

II. Visibility and Transparency is the result of seeing no Separation between God and self. The Divine becomes all-at-once indivisible from any other soul.

III. We are all one and what we fail to do for ourselves, we fail to do for another.

Learning Objectives:

You will learn how to believe in your own power.

4 – Exercises

***Conversations with God book 2*, Chapter 20- Affirmation**

"I believe in my own power to change. I will not give my power away to anyone or anything."

---

1. Take a moment to write down in your journal what you believe about:
   - God
   - Love
   - Success
   - Failure
   - Work
   - Money
   - Women
   - Men
   - Sex

2. If you have negative, or rather destructive or counter-productive beliefs about some of these categories, think about how you could change this non-productive belief into a pro-life, spiritual-building belief.

   Examples:
   - If you believe that God is going to punish you for your sins, switch that destructive thought by writing down, "God will always love you, no matter what."
   - If you believe that you are not allowed to fail, switch that negative thought by writing down that you forgive yourself lovingly for any outcome you ever had in your life.

3. At first, even if you don't believe in a constructive, positive thought, write it down. It will start planting a seed in your awareness. Keep focused on building change for yourself.

4. Now choose a partner and share your discoveries with each other.

KEY DEFINITIONS for Chapter 20:

Religion: set of beliefs, traditions and practices, often centered upon specific moral claims about reality, the cosmos, and human nature, and often codified as prayer, ritual, dogma, and religious law. Religion also encompasses ancestral or cultural traditions, writings, history, and mythology, as well as personal faith and mystic experience. The term "religion" refers to both the personal practices related to communal faith and to group rituals and communication stemming from shared conviction.

Spirituality: concerns itself with matters of the spirit or soul. Spiritual matters are those matters regarding humankind's earthly nature and purpose; encompasses not only biological but as beings with a unique relationship to that which is beyond time and space.

5 – Summary of this chapter lesson:

- Embracing our cultures and religion and going beyond the biological, the physical brings us back to spirituality.

- In your experience of switching negative beliefs into positive ones, what have you learned about yourself? How do you think it will change future generations?

- Dialogue with your partner or community groups: How will what we believe affect our world's future?

CLOSING WORD

For almost twenty years I worked for a corporation in United States, toiling long hours and wondering what was my life's meaning. To answer this inner question, I started a deep introspection and I found that a full and complete life is not possible without struggle. Liberation and struggle are part of everyday life. This is the Law of Opposites, lived.

Neale Donald Walsch, in his *Conversations with God* book series, gives us a complete guideline on leading a peaceful life for a better world. I see this world clearly – a vision that takes into consideration all human beings, a world that is compassionate, loving and caring *for the good of all.*

The exercises and tools provided in this Guidebook are very powerful. I sincerely hope that you have been able to see and feel deeply some benefits from them all. I have practiced all of the techniques described and my life has completely changed. I am now living my dreams and attracting more of what I desire. You can live all of your dreams as well, by transcending ordinary struggle into an extraordinary life, filled with inner bliss.

Namaste.

Kindly Contact:

SNS, Inc.
After Hours Programs, Retreats, Camps, Trainings, & Materials
for
Youth and their Adult Leaders
Ages 3-103 !

~ School of the New Spirituality ~
Correspondence Office
Post Office Box 622
Tyrone, Georgia 30290
USA
www.SchooloftheNewSpirituality.com

Info@SchooloftheNewSpirituality.com

~ Leadership, Community-Building Kits ~
SNSatlanta@yahoo.com

~ Parent Pathway Team & Eyes Wide Open Store ~
Laurie@SchooloftheNewSpirituality.com

~ SNS Communications, Website & Community Postings ~
Alecia@SchooloftheNewSpirituality.com

~ SNS Dallas & FREE2BU Parent Empowerment Kits ~
Angel@SchooloftheNewSpirituality.com

"Other New Spirituality Principles as shared through Neale's other books"

New Spirituality Principles

Enumerated within the *Conversation with God* books
— many principles are featured in more than one *Conversations with God* title —

The Three Statements of Ultimate Truth are:

1. We are all one.
2. There's enough.
3. There's nothing you have to do.

---

3 Core Concepts of Holistic Living—Living as a Whole Person—Body-Mind-Spirit

Awareness—Honesty—Responsibility used to:

1. Redefine yourself as individuals
2. Redefine yourself as a society
3. Redefine "success"

These replace the 3 P's:
    Productivity
    Popularity
    Possessions

---

5 Fallacies about God

1. God needs something.
2. God can fail to get what God needs.
3. God has separated you from God because you have not given God what God needs.
4. God still needs what God needs so badly that God now requires you, from your separated position, to provide it.
5. God will destroy you if you do not meet God's requirements.

---

5 Fallacies about Life

1. Human beings are separate from each other.
2. There is not enough of what human beings need to be happy.
3. To get the stuff of which there is not enough, human beings must compete with each other.
4. Some human beings are better than other human beings.
5. It is appropriate for human beings to resolve severe differences created by all the other fallacies by killing each other.

Characteristics of *Tomorrow's God*

1. Tomorrow's God does not require anyone to believe in God.

2. Tomorrow's God is without gender, size, shape, color, or any of the characteristics of an individual living being.

3. Tomorrow's God talks with everyone, all the time

4. Tomorrow's God is separate from nothing, but is Everywhere Present, the All In All, the Alpha and the Omega, the Beginning and the End, the Sum Total of Everything that ever was, is now, and ever shall be.

5. Tomorrow's God is not a singular Super Being, but the extraordinary process called Life.

6. Tomorrow's God is ever changing.

7. Tomorrow's God is needless.

8. Tomorrow's God does not ask to be served, but is the Servant of all of Life.

9. Tomorrow's God will be unconditionally loving, nonjudgmental, non-condemning, and non-punishing.

Principles of the New Spirituality (*New Revelations*)

1. God has never stopped communicating directly with human beings. God has been communicating with and through human beings from the beginning of time. God does so today.

2. Every human being is as special as every other human being who has ever lived, lives now, or ever will live. You are all messengers. Every one of you. You are carrying a message to life about life every day. Every hour. Every moment.

3. No path to God is more direct than any other path. No religion is the "one true religion," no people are "the chosen people," and no prophet is the "greatest prophet."

4. God needs nothing. God requires nothing in order to be happy. God is happiness itself. Therefore, God requires nothing of anyone or anything in the Universe.

5. God is not a singular Super Being, living somewhere in the Universe or outside of it, having the same emotional needs and subject to the same emotional turmoil as humans. That Which Is God cannot be hurt or damaged in any way, and so, has no need to seek revenge or impose punishment.

6. All things are One Thing. There is only One Thing, and all things are part of the One Thing That Is.

7. There is no such thing as Right and Wrong. There is only What Works and What Does Not Work, depending upon what it is that you seek to be, do, or have.

8. You are not your body. Who You Are is limitless and without end.

9. You cannot die, and you will never be condemned to eternal damnation.

The 3 Basic Life Principles
1. Functionality
2. Adaptability
3. Sustainability

Which replace: Morality - Justice - Ownership

The New Gospel:

"We are all One."

"Ours is not a better way, ours is merely another way."

Be-Do-Have Paradigm

The "Be-Do-Have Paradigm" is a way of looking at life. It is nothing more or less than that. Yet this way of looking at life could change your life—and probably will. Because what is true about this paradigm is that most people have it all backward, and when they finally get it straightened out and start looking at it frontward, everything in their lives shifts 180-degrees. NDW writes:

> Most people (I know I did) started out with the understanding that how life worked was like this: Have-Do-Be. That is, when I HAVE the right stuff, I can DO the right things, and then I will get to BE what I want to be.
>
> When I HAVE good grades I can DO the thing called graduate and I can BE the thing called employable—might be one example. Here's another. When I HAVE enough money I can DO the thing called buy a house and I can BE the thing called secure. Want one more? Here goes: When I HAVE enough time I can DO the thing called take a vacation and I can BE the thing called rested and relaxed.
>
> See how it works? This is how my father, my school, my society told me that it works. Life works this way. The only problem was, I was NOT getting to BE the things I thought I was going to get to be after I had done all that I thought I had to do, and had all the things that I thought I needed to have. Or, if I did get to BE that, I only got to be it for a short period of time. Soon after I got to be "happy" or "secure" or "contented," or whatever it was that I thought I was going to get to be, I found myself once again UNhappy, INsecure, and NOT contented ! I didn't seem to know how to "hold onto the stuff." I didn't know how to make the flavor last. So it always seemed as if I did all that I had to do for nothing. It felt like wasted effort, and I began to resent that in my life.
>
> Then I had the *Conversations with God* experience, and everything changed. God told me that I was starting out in the wrong place. What I needed to do was BEGIN where I thought I was going to GO.
>
> All creation starts from a place of BEING, God said, and I have had it in the reverse. The trick in life is not to try to get to be "happy," or be "secure," or whatever, but to start out BEING happy, or BEING content, of whatever, and go from there in the living of our daily lives.
>
> But how do you do that if you don't HAVE what you NEED TO HAVE in order to be happy, etc.? That's the question, and it's a fair one. The answer is that coming FROM a state of being, rather than trying to get TO a state of being, practically assures that the "havingness" end of the equation is taken care of.
>
> When you come FROM a state of being, you need to have nothing in order to begin the process. You simply select, quite arbitrarily, a state of being, and then come from that place in everything you think, say, and do. But because you are thinking, saying, and doing only what a person who is being happy, contented, or whatever, thinks, says and does, the things that a happy or contented person winds up HAVING come to you automatically.
>
> Let's try this out and see if it really can work that way. Let's say that what a person wants to BE is the thing called "secure." If that is the desired experience, what we can do is start OUT from the square on the playing board that says, I AM SECURE. We start out with this idea, and this is the operating idea behind everything we do. We have moved into the BE-DO portion of the paradigm.

When a person does what only a secure person would do, that person almost automatically winds up having what only a secure person would have. Try it out some-time. It's amazing how this works.

The 5 Attitudes of Godliness

1. Joy
2. Love
3. Acceptance
4. Blessing
5. Gratitude

The Prime Value
Life itself is the Prime Value

This replaces the world's definition that the Prime Value is power

The Triad Process

1. Nothing in my world is real.
2. The meaning of everything is the meaning I give it.
3. I am who I say I am, and my experience is what I say it is.

5 Steps to Peace

Step 1   Acknowledge that some of your old beliefs about God and about Life are no longer working.

Step 2   Acknowledge that there is something you do not understand about God and about Life, the understanding of which will change everything.

Step 3   Be willing for a new understanding of God and Life to now be brought forth, an understanding that could produce a new way of life on this planet.

Step 4   Be courageous enough to explore and examine this new understanding, and, if it aligns with your inner truth and knowing, to enlarge your belief system to include it.

Step 5   Choose to live your life as a demonstration of your highest and grandest beliefs, rather than as denials of them

7 interchangeable words for God:

Love
Life
Joy
Peace
Freedom
Change
You (Me, Us)

The 5 Levels of Truth-telling

1. Tell the truth to yourself about yourself.
2. Tell the truth to yourself about another.
3. Tell the truth about yourself to another.
4. Tell the truth about another to that other.
5. Tell the truth to everyone about everything.

The Seven Steps to *Friendship with God* are:

Know God
Trust God
Love God
Embrace God
Use God
Help God
Thank God

Tools of Creation

1. Thought
2. Word
3. Action

The Divine Dichotomy

By moving from an either/or world to a both/and world, I see that both "this" and "that" can be true at the same time, and that allows me to see much more of how things really are in the world around me.

Example: is the rain good or bad? Desert or flood?

The Ten Illusions

1. Need Exists
2. Failure Exists
3. Disunity Exists
4. Insufficiency Exists
5. Requirement Exists
6. Judgment Exists
7. Condemnation Exists
8. Conditionality Exists
9. Superiority Exists
10. Ignorance Exists

These illusions have created humanity's cultural story, from which our present difficulties emerge. The cultural story of humans is that …

1. God has an agenda. (Need Exists)

2. The outcome of life is in doubt. (Failure Exists)

3. You are separate from God. (Disunity Exists)

4. There is not enough. (Insufficiency Exists)

5. There is something you have to do. (Requirement Exists)

6. If you do not do it, you will be punished. (Judgment Exists)

7. The punishment is everlasting damnation. (Condemnation Exists)

8. Love is, therefore, conditional. (Conditionality Exists)

9. Knowing and meeting the conditions renders you superior. (Superiority Exists)

10. You do not know that these are illusions. (Ignorance Exists)

The 18 Remembrances from *Home with God, in a Life that Never Ends*

1) Dying is something you do for you.

2) You are the cause of your own death. This is always true, no matter where, or how, you die.

3) You cannot die against your will.

4)   No path back Home is better than any other path.

5)   Death is never a tragedy. It is always a gift.

6)   You and God are one. There is no separation between you.

7)   Death does not exist.

8)   You can't change Ultimate Reality, but you *can* change your experience of it.

9)   It is the desire of All That Is to Know Itself in its own Experience. This is the reason for all of Life.

10) Life is eternal.

11) The timing and the circumstances of death are always perfect.

12) The death of every person always serves the agenda of every other person who is aware of it. *That is why they are aware of it.* Therefore, no death (and no life) is ever "wasted." No one ever dies "in vain."

13) Birth and death are the same thing.

14) You are continually in the act of creation, in life and in death.

15) There is no such thing as the end of evolution.

16) Death is reversible.

17) In death you will be greeted by all of your loved ones—those who have died before you and those who will die after you.

18) Free Choice is the act of pure creation, the signature of God, and your gift, your glory, and your power forever and ever.

School of the New Spirituality
Youth People's Programs
and Programs for Leaders of Youth, ages 3-103 !

The School of the New Spirituality's curricula, materials, and programs promote, empower, and enable love—love of self, family, friends, and community (local to global). Developing a loving peace inside you can create great joy; such inner caring and peace actually shifts the world to a different energy level. A personal 'peace moment' is a fundamental building block to world peace. Self-love leads to a compassion and understanding of our humanity, our commonalities with others, of all living beings, and our ONEness as spiritual beings having an earthly experience.

To contact

School of the New Spirituality, Inc.

Retreats, Camps, Trainings, Interactive Materials and Fun Kits
for
Children and their Leaders

SNS, Inc.
Post Office Box 622
Tyrone, Georgia 30290
USA

About the Author

Anne-Marie Barbier was born in Paris, France, and attended private schools in Tunisia, Algeria and Madagascar due to her father's international assignments. Anne-Marie earned a BAC in Business and Office Administration in France. Anne-Marie's professional work experience includes five years as general director of a restaurant in Port Grimaud, France; followed by six years in marketing and sales for several women's fashion retail stores in Saint-Tropez, France, and the Turks and Caicos Islands. From 1985 to 2003, Anne Marie worked for big corporations in United States and was involved in every aspect of marketing, media relations, customer service, management, employees/ team-building, and leadership training.

While conducting training and researching management and leadership theory, Anne-Marie discovered Dr. Deepak Chopra's writings. In 2002 she became certified by the Chopra Center for Well Being to teach a workshop titled "The Seven Universal Laws of Success in the Workplace." In 2004, Anne-Marie was certified to instruct Primordial Sound Meditation and in 2005 she earned her certification to teach the Seven Spiritual Laws of Yoga from the Chopra Center for Well Being in California.

During the last few years in Atlanta, Anne-Marie was self-employed as a yoga, meditation and spirituality workshop instructor. In November 2005, she relocated to France where she has opened her Yoga Institute, Milles Petales. She is a board member of the School of the New Spirituality and is leading monthly book clubs on the material in the *Conversations with God* books by Neale Donald Walsch. She serves as secretary of the Toulon area Lion's Club, where she is very active in working for the community, speaking, and organizing business development activities and education.

She is proud to be an American citizen since June 1995. See her bio and workshop posted on the School of the New Spirituality website by clicking "About Us" and "Workshops." She may be reached at her email: Blissofspirit9@cs.com .

PHOTOS: (1) Anne-Marie Barbier
(2) Anne-Marie's yoga pose alpha, at her Yoga Institute
(3) David and Linda Ratto with Anne-Marie, in Atlanta

END NOTES

For deeper study and reference:

Beatles: "Love, Love, Love. Love, Love, Love. Love is all you need."
           Google: "Beatles" for more lyrics and poetry about Love.

Neale Donald Walsch
    Conversations with God books – www.nealedonaldwalsch.com and
    www.SchooloftheNewSpirituality.com

Deepak Chopra, MD, *Everyday Immortality*
Deepak Chopra, *The Spontaneous Fulfillment of Desire*
Deepak Chopra, *The Seven Spiritual Laws of Success*
Deepak Chopra, *Peace is the Way*
Deepak Chopra, *The Path to Love*
Deepak Chopra, *Life After Death*
    www.chopra.com

Eckhart Tolle, *The Power of Now* and also: *The New Earth*
    www.eckharttolle.com

Wayne Dyer, *The Power of Intention*
    www.drwaynedyer.com

David Simon, *Wisdom of Healing*
    David Simon, *The Ten Commitments*
    www.chopra.com

Louise Hay, *You Can Heal Your Life*
    www.louisehay.com

Marshall Rosenberg, PhD, *Nonviolent Communication*
    www.cnvc.com

Gandhi, *An Autobiography*
    www.mkgandhi.com

Durkheim, Emile, *The Division of Labour (1893)*
    The Rules of Sociological Method (1895)
    Suicide (1897)
    The Elementary Forms of Religious Life (1912)
    www.emile-durkheim.com

Sautet Marc
    Nietzsche for Beginners (1986)
    www.cafe-philo-desphares.info

James Twyman, *The Moses Code*
    www.jamestwyman.com and www.belovedcommunity.com

INDEX

A

Abraham Maslow, 104
Adi Shankara, 34
Alternative, 41, 57, 59
Anger, 70, 71
Archetypes, 34
Attitude, v, 74, 76
Awareness, v, 38, 39, 45, 93, 96, 103, 117
Ayurveda, 22, 24, 25, 32

C

Carl Jung, 102
Choice, 124
Chopra, Deepak, ix, xi, 2, 8, 13, 17, 21, 34, 63, 68, 69, 77, 85, 94, 103, 110, 127, 129
Churchill, Winston, 68
Commitment, 3
Communication, 86, 87, 129
Comparison Chart, 41
Consciousness, v, 20, 28, 34, 39, 73, 93
Creativity, 39

D

David Simon, 25, 74, 129
Deepak Chopra, ix, xi, 2, 8, 13, 17, 21, 34, 63, 68, 69, 77, 85, 94, 103, 110, 127, 129
Divine, iii, v, xiii, xv, 3, 21, 30, 34, 39, 70, 109, 110, 122
Doing, 103, 105
Dyer, Wayne, 8, 129

E

Eckhart Tolle, 2, 8, 13, 129
Education, iv, v, 37, 43, 45, 59, 61
Ego, 34, 104
Enlightenment, 1, 33
Emerson, 104
Empowerment, v, 82, 103, 115
Energy, 23, 31

F

Freedom, 122

G

Gandhi, 38, 68, 87, 90, 129
God, iii, v, vii, ix, xiii, 1, 2, 3, 5, 7, 9, 10, 13, 14, 17, 18, 21, 22, 23, 25, 26, 29, 30, 33, 35, 38, 39, 41, 45, 55, 57, 59, 63, 64, 67, 68, 69, 70, 73, 74, 77, 78, 81, 85, 86, 89, 90, 91, 93, 94, 98, 99, 100, 101, 102, 103, 107, 109, 110, 111, 113, 117, 118, 119, 120, 121, 122, 123, 124, 127, 129, 133, 134, 135, 136, 137, 138, 139, 140, 141, 142, 143, 144, 145, 146, 147, 148, 149, 150, 151, 152
Government, 93
Gratitude, 15, 121

H

Happiness, 91
Hay, Louise, 29, 129
Help, v, 43, 81, 82, 122
Hostility, 71

I

Intentions, 45

J

James Twyman, 86, 129
Jung, Carl, 102

K

Karma, 21, 24
Krishnamurti, 103

L

Leaders, 57, 86, 87, 115, 125
Louise Hay, 29, 129
Love, v, 29, 30, 68, 74, 77, 78, 85, 93, 96, 106, 111, 121, 122, 123, 129

M

Marshall B. Rosenberg, 86
Maslow, Abraham, 104
Meditation, ix, 34, 35, 127
Milles Petales, 127
mind, 33, 34, 39, 57, 73, 117
Miracles, 2, 3
mirror, xv, 15, 16, 31, 91, 104
Moses Code, The, 86, 129
Mother Theresa, 87, 95

My Own Conversation with God

My Own Conversation with God

_____

_____

_____

_____

_____

_____

_____

_____

_____

_____

_____

_____

_____

_____

_____

_____

_____

_____

_____

_____

_____

_____

_____

_____

_____

_____

_____

_____

My Own Conversation with God

My Own Conversation with God

_____

_____

_____

_____

_____

_____

_____

_____

_____

_____

_____

_____

_____

_____

_____

_____

_____

_____

_____

_____

_____

_____

_____

_____

_____

_____

_____

_____

_____

My Own Conversation with God

My Own Conversation with God

_____

_____

_____

_____

_____

_____

_____

_____

_____

_____

_____

_____

_____

_____

_____

_____

_____

_____

_____

_____

_____

_____

_____

_____

_____

_____

_____

My Own Conversation with God

_____

_____

_____

_____

_____

_____

_____

_____

_____

_____

_____

_____

_____

_____

_____

_____

_____

_____

_____

_____

_____

_____

_____

_____

_____

_____

_____

_____

_____

_____

_____

_____

My Own Conversation with God

_____

_____

_____

_____

_____

_____

_____

_____

_____

_____

_____

_____

_____

_____

_____

_____

_____

_____

_____

_____

_____

_____

_____

_____

_____

_____

_____

_____

My Own Conversation with God

_____

_____

_____

_____

_____

_____

_____

_____

_____

_____

_____

_____

_____

_____

_____

_____

_____

_____

_____

_____

_____

_____

_____

_____

_____

_____

_____

_____

_____

_____

My Own Conversation with God

_____

_____

_____

_____

_____

_____

_____

_____

_____

_____

_____

_____

_____

_____

_____

_____

_____

_____

_____

_____

_____

_____

_____

_____

_____

_____

_____

_____

My Own Conversation with God

_____

_____

_____

_____

_____

_____

_____

_____

_____

_____

_____

_____

_____

_____

_____

_____

_____

_____

_____

_____

_____

_____

_____

_____

_____

_____

_____

_____

_____

My Own Conversation with God

My Own Conversation with God

_____

_____

_____

_____

_____

_____

_____

_____

_____

_____

_____

_____

_____

_____

_____

_____

_____

_____

_____

_____

_____

_____

_____

_____

_____

_____

_____

My Own Conversation with God

_____

_____

_____

_____

_____

_____

_____

_____

_____

_____

_____

_____

_____

_____

_____

_____

_____

_____

_____

_____

_____

_____

_____

_____

_____

_____

_____

_____

_____

_____

My Own Conversation with God

My Own Conversation with God

_____

_____

_____

_____

_____

_____

_____

_____

_____

_____

_____

_____

_____

_____

_____

_____

_____

_____

_____

_____

_____

_____

_____

_____

_____

My Own Conversation with God

_____

_____

_____

_____

_____

_____

_____

_____

_____

_____

_____

_____

_____

_____

_____

_____

_____

_____

_____

_____

_____

_____

_____

_____

_____

_____

_____

My Own Conversation with God

_____
_____
_____
_____
_____
_____
_____
_____
_____
_____
_____
_____
_____
_____
_____
_____
_____
_____
_____
_____
_____
_____
_____
_____
_____
_____
_____
_____

My Own Conversation with God

_____

_____

_____

_____

_____

_____

_____

_____

_____

_____

_____

_____

_____

_____

_____

_____

_____

_____

_____

_____

_____

_____

_____

_____

_____

_____

_____

_____

Printed in the United States
148299LV00001B/28/P